Hummingbirds
of
North America:
Attracting,
Feeding,
and
Photographing

Hummingbirds
of
North America:
Attracting,
Feeding,
and
Photographing

Dan True

University of New Mexico Press
Albuquerque

Library of Congress Cataloging-in-Publication Data

True, Dan, 1924–
    Hummingbirds of North America: attracting,
  feeding, and photographing / Dan True—1st ed.
     p. cm.
    Includes bibliographical reference (p.) and index.
    ISBN 0-8263-1398-1 (cloth)
    Paperbound ISBN: 0-8263-1608-5
    1. Hummingbirds—North America.   2. Birds,
Attracting of.   I. Title.
QL696.A558T78   1993
598'.899—dc20   93-21709
                                       CIP

Contents

Contents

Preface

This book provides information that hasn't been previously published about hummingbirds. Additionally, there are color photographs of both male and female hummingbirds known to nest in North America. These photographs make species comparisons and identification easier. Biographical sketches of each species accompany the photographs.

Hummingbird navigation and migration is written from my experience as a meteorologist, and as a pilot on flights over the birds' migration routes through Mexico, the United States, and Canada. In some areas I have made balloon flights over hummingbird migration routes to observe their habits; sometimes the little birds darted about the balloon, often pausing to hover and examine points of red on the craft. I feel fortunate to observe and write about hummingbirds, almost from their own viewpoints.

Along with accounts of how and what to feed hummingbirds, there are opinions presented as to whether feeding is good or bad for them. This book also includes a detailed look at feeder designs; hummingbird predators; ways to control uninvited guests at feeders; an account of how to photograph hummingbirds; a history of the hummingbird feeder, and more.

Introduction

Hummingbirds captured my attention by way of a female golden eagle in Texas. One April morning, I sat in a small photo blind atop a house-sized flat boulder down in the panhandle's Palo Duro Canyon. My cameras were poised, awaiting action in an eagle's cliff nest. Mesquite, cholla cactus, yucca, and juniper grew in the canyon. A hundred yards to my right was the edge of a stand of tall red cedar covering several acres on lush ground watered by small springs oozing from the canyon's walls. Behind me a quarter of a mile, sunshine sparkled a ribbon of rippling water meandering along the canyon's grassy floor. From the direction of the stream a wild turkey gobbled. In the canyon's solitude I idly imagined the contrast between an eagle and a hummingbird. Then my mind's eye pictured a wild eagle and a hummingbird, in the same photograph. But hummingbirds in that semi-arid, rocky canyon? Not likely, I thought. Yet . . .

Off and on I had spent twenty years in Palo Duro Canyon. Eight of those I lived in the ranch headquarters house of a 16,000-acre spread that included much of the canyon. Throughout that time I saw only two hummingbirds; one was perched on our chicken lot fence; the second briefly hummed around the head of a female golden eagle I was raising (True 1989). Both sightings I dismissed as stray migrants that might have been blown off course by unusual weather.

From inside my blind I replayed the idea of an eagle-hummer photograph. I dislike projects with low success odds, but at the same time, the photo idea inspired my curiosity about hummingbirds. I pulled a worn Peterson's bird field guide from my pack and flipped to the section on hummingbirds.

According to the guide, hummingbirds seasonally populate every one of the lower forty-eight states, plus most of Canada and Alaska . . . intriguing.

On my next trip to town I bought a hummingbird feeder. On the way back to the canyon I paused at Amarillo's public library and researched the ratio of sugar to water recommended for feeding hummingbirds: one part sugar to four parts water, boiled two minutes and cooled. Before leaving the library I scanned a copy of *Palo Duro Canyon Bird Checklist*. No hummingbirds were listed. (Current Palo Duro Canyon checklists include them.)

Male Ruby-Throated with pollen on head.

Down in the canyon I half-heartedly filled the new feeder. Prompted by the photo idea, I suspended the feeder at the end of a three-foot bare cedar limb in front of my blind. The branch pointed toward the cliff in such a way that the eagle's nest formed the feeder's background. I reset one camera for the imagined eagle-hummer photo and settled in for what my skeptical side thought might be a long wait.

For weeks the eagles came and went. During that time evening showers wet the countryside. Mesquite greened, and clumps of wild-flowers and cacti blossomed. Locusts and other insects emerged, and Mississippi kites, along with many other birds, returned to the canyon from wintering grounds somewhere far to the south. Although I saw no hummingbirds, I cleaned the feeder and recharged it with fresh mixture every three or four days. As days passed, disappointment replaced optimism, and I gradually let go of the eagle-hummingbird photo idea. Then, one afternoon near the middle of May, a male Black-chinned whizzed to the feeder and hovered, as if studying the device. Three feet in front of my eyes the perky little bird's tiny wings fanned the Texas air.

2

Introduction

Eagerly, the hummingbird poked its tongue up and down and around the feeder without finding its feeding ports. Obviously hungry, the little fellow jabbed at sticky areas he discovered on the device. From his behavior I sensed it was his first encounter with an artificial feeder. The bird soon figured out how the gadget worked, and drank from it a long time without pause. By evening, the Black-chinned had become a regular visitor. At sundown he drank an especially long time, and disappeared into the canyon's gloom. I hoped he would be back the next day.

At sunrise the hummingbird was feeding when I returned to the blind. All day he came to the feeder regularly. I loved the way this mite of a bird zipped in, screeched to a mid-air halt, fed until sated, and zipped away. He had style, and it occurred to me that if a person were depressed, it would be difficult to remain so while watching hummingbirds.

A few days after the Black-chinned arrived, a red-gorgeted male Broad-tailed buzzed in and fed as if he was an old hand at feeders. Next day a couple of females of both varieties joined the males.

Mid-air squabbling broke out around the feeder. The birds "displayed" at each other by spreading tail feathers and pitching wing feathers to maximize buzz. I admired their happy go-get-'em confidence. Gram for gram, hummingbirds had more personality than anything in the canyon. To make life easier for them I placed a second feeder on the other side of my blind. Posturing and bluffing continued, but the birds seemed more at ease.

Next day the Broad-tails disappeared. My field guide said this species commonly nests in the Rocky Mountains. I assumed they had tanked up at my feeder before flying on. Meanwhile, the little Black-chinned hens darted through the air, occasionally trailing cobwebs into sparse undergrowth near my blind. I assumed they were preparing to nest.

The boulder my photo blind was on lay about a hundred yards from a small spring. Hummingbird travel in that direction was frequent. (Later I discovered the hummers bathing and playing in its waters.) By mid-June, when the young eagles had grown and fledged, my photo blind feeder was the hub of a hummingbird traffic jam. Although the eagle-hummingbird photograph never materialized, my interest in hummingbirds was irretrievably launched.

After the eagle project was finished, I visited southern Arizona's Mile Hi/Ramsey Canyon Preserve, considered by some to be the hummingbird capital of North America. From there I studied and filmed hummingbirds in Madera Canyon south of Tucson; the Spofford bird sanctuary near Portal, Arizona; the Chiricahua and Huachuca mountains of southeast Arizona; the Guadalupe mountains of southeast Arizona and southwest New Mexico; Tucker Wildlife Sanctuary in Modjeska Canyon east of Orange, California; most Mexican provinces that serve as wintering grounds for North American hummingbirds, including Tzintzuntzan, which translates "Place of the Hummingbirds," and pronounces to imitate the sound of a hovering hummingbird; and the southern half of Vancouver Island, British Columbia, Canada. I also began attending the annual Hummer/Bird Celebrations at Rockport-Fulton, Texas. And for years I have worked with the array of hummingbird varieties found in North America and Mexico. Additionally, I have met with hummingbird experts across the United States, and joined in hummingbird banding operations. At various universities, I have taken courses in biology, geography, horticulture, and natural history. These studies and travels, plus my 3,500 hours as a commercial pilot, along with several years as a meteorologist, have helped me see the world from a hummingbird's viewpoint.

All About
Hummers

Natural Attractions

Flowers are probably the hummingbird's single most important attention grabber, providing nectar (sugar) that birds convert into energy for powering muscles. Texas has more varieties of wildflowers than any other state in the Union, and more species of hummingbirds than any other state—nineteen out of the twenty-four kinds that have been verified in the United States.

Is it true that red is the only color hummingbirds see? Hummingbirds have an exploring attitude that drives them to search for new sources of nectar. I've seen young hummingbirds investigate objects of various colors, including aluminum wind chimes. When filming Broad-tails, a male and female fed simultaneously from a minature jet black Indian wedding vase I used for a special photograph. Tests, however, indicate that hummingbird eyes more readily separate reds from other colors. And generally, flowers that produce nectar in sugar ratios hummingbirds prefer are red or shades of red. This suggests the bird's attraction to red may be a learned response.

Three top-of-the-line-flowers to attract hummers in any area are common trumpet creeper, twinberry (Lonicera involucrata), and the columbines. Also known as trumpet vine and trumpet honeysuckle, native trumpet creeper (*Bignonia radicans*), contains ten times more nectar than average wild flowers, making it the richest hummingbird flower in North America. (Conversation with Dr. Peter Scott, Arizona State University 1991). Native trumpet creeper flowers are smaller than hybrid varieties, and therefore easier for the birds to feed from. Male hummingbirds become very possessive of a trumpet creeper flower patch.

Of the columbines, reds are the most popular with hummers: *Aquilegia formosa* and *A. elegams* in the western U.S. and Canada; *Aquilegia canadensis* in the eastern U.S. and Canada. Other hummingbird flowers include the following:

azaleas	fuchsia	geraniums
scarlet penstemon	cardinal flower	scarlet salvia
scarlet morning glory	fire pink	bee balm
cypress vine	scarlet petunia	scarlet paintbrush

geiger tree	red buckeye	scarlet bush
coral bells	bouvardia	tobacco tree
honeysuckle	impatiens	petunia

Generally, flowers known as hummingbird flowers have little or no fragrance. Rather than waste energy on producing odor, hummingbird flowers apparently direct their energy toward making themselves visible, and producing nectar. Smell tests performed on hummingbirds indicate the birds have practically no sense of smell (Stong 1960). Also, flowers that have developed corollas encouraging pollination by hummingbirds tend to be daytime bloomers, usually blooming over a longer span of time than insect pollinated flowers.

An item to remember when selecting flowers for hummers is that most cultivated hybrids, which include many garden flowers, usually produce significantly less nectar than nonhybrids. Also, an assortment of flowers with staggered blossomings will give the birds a longer time to feed "in the wild."

Mosquitoes, gnats, and fruit flies also get a hummingbird's attention. Nourishment from these insects provides protein for feather, bone, and muscle maintenance and growth. To see hummingbirds hawking insects on the wing is a sight. Often the birds will hover within or on the fringe of an airborne insect swarm, gracefully pirouetting while zapping insects out of the air with a flick of the tongue. In this regard, hummingbirds are miniature flycatchers. The birds also glean insects, especially small spiders, from shrubs, tree bark, and under the eaves of buildings. According to testing by the late Dr. Augusto Ruschi, the Brazilian hummingbird expert, a hummingbird eats ten to fifteen gnats, flies, mosquitoes, or spiders per day.

If you live in an apartment, a porch or railing flower planter will make a successful hummingbird attractor. I've had reports of hummingbirds coming to feeders on the upper floors of high-rise buildings. After watching the birds feed from flowers growing on near-vertical walls of Mexico's tropical mountains, a hummingbird's apparently easy adaptation to scaling high-rise structures figures.

Consistently, larger numbers of hummingbirds occur in urban areas with an abundance of trees and shrubs. One reason could be that trees and shrubs harbor insects. Other reasons may be that trees offer a place to perch, which is how hummingbirds spend 80 percent of their day; trees and shrubs provide refuge from predators and shelter from winds and severe thunderstorms. (The little rascals regularly fly in "normal" rains.)

Migration

If you have few trees, the birds must have alternative perches. Clotheslines, power lines, etc., preferably near feeders, will increase your chance of luring birds.

Once hummingbirds are attracted by flowers, trees, insects, or perches, their curiosity will automatically lead them to discover feeders. Keep in mind, however, that if seasonal weather has favored the flower world's prosperity, hummingbirds will feed less at feeders. If flowers are in a slump, the birds will visit feeders more often (Inouye et. al. 1991). Spring flowers, in fact, seem to control when and at what pace the birds make migration moves. Where do they come from, and how does such a small bird fly great distances?

Migration

Prime hummingbird attraction time is during spring migration. Early migrants of some species arrive from Mexico in the extreme southern United States as early as January or February. Others arrive in March and April.

Hummingbird migration hinges on two items: flower nectar and insects. The birds need carbohydrates (sugar) to energize muscles so they can hum around and catch insects (protein) for body growth and maintenance.

After flowers bloom, insect availability that follows apparently controls hummingbird arrivals. Friends and I have noted that spring's first insect eating swallows are often followed a day or two later by hummingbirds.

In years when spring flower growth is normal in Mexico and the southern United States, hummingbirds migrate at a normal pace and in normal numbers. From year to year, an increase or decrease in flowers correspondingly affects yearly hummingbird numbers. In the southwest, in years when rain or snow has been ideal and the desert is alive with flowers, few birds frequent feeders as long as the flowers bloom. Hummingbirds seem to remain in a desert rich with flowers, rather than flying to feeders filled with "cheap stuff."

Natural enroute stopover time for the birds is from seven to fourteen days (Carpenter et al. 1983). During a stop in spring, if hummingbirds find what they need, chances are they will extend their visit into summer. Therefore, it is wise to have feeders in place a week before birds are expected, in case of early arrivals. (Refer to the State/ Province List for your area's spring and fall migration dates.) If an early spring brings forth flowers and insects, I would hang a feeder early, regardless of the calendar. Since a four-to-one water-sugar solution doesn't freeze until cooled to 24° F, mild freezes should be no problem.

As spring advances and flowers blossom in a northward progression, the birds ride the crest of the flower-insect wave. For example, the National Wildflower Research Center near Austin, Texas, sees hummingbird numbers peak during the period of greatest flowering, mid-April to mid-May.

Hummingbirds also seem to ride tail winds. It has been my experience that the wind is from a southern quadrant when our first Black-chins arrive at my home in Albuquerque from southern wintering grounds. Observers have also noted at Hawk Mountain, Pennsylvania, that Ruby-throated hummingbird sightings in fall increase with winds favorable to the direction the birds wish to move (Willimont et al. 1988). And during fall migration in the Rockport-Fulton area of Texas, birders have noted that tail winds dramatically increase the numbers of Ruby-throats navigating along the coast toward Mexico.

Invariably, mature male hummingbirds arrive ahead of females, by as much as three weeks in the spring. In the fall, just as invariably, mature males fly south ahead of females and young ones. There may be good reason for this male-female migration sequence.

Hummingbirds are on an energy tightrope. To meet their energy needs, the birds visit between two thousand and five thousand flowers per day (personal conversation with Dr. Peter Scott). Obviously, a hummingbird must be no more than minutes away from a food source throughout its life. During migration, the birds are faced with the additional problem of locating food at some unknown place in the distance. As a hummingbird survival strategy, it may be that nature encourages mature males to lead in the hazardous task of bridging gaps between food sources. In this way, if a male fails to find nourishment before his reserves are exhausted and he dies, the hummingbird world loses only a male bird. On the other hand, when males successfully locate a food source bridging a migration energy gap, their colorful, high visibility feeding on the wing provides winking signs that steer females and their trailing youngsters to food, and survival. Apparently it is more efficient to risk males than to endanger females and youngsters on chancy food searches during migration. Evidence that male hummingbirds lose their lives more often than females comes from Dr. William Calder's banding research. Calder's records indicate that female hummingbirds live an average of three and a half years, while males average only two and a half. The difference in male-female average life spans tends to support reasoning for the male-female migration sequence. This could make an interesting in-depth study, through examination of banding records that tabulate male/female/young ratios at specific times. (The surplus of females could also help explain why male hummingbirds often mate with more than one female.)

You can easily judge when an individual bird is about to migrate or resume migration. In California, 17 miles northwest of Bishop, migrating Rufous hummingbirds fed more often and longer an hour before departure (Carpenter et al. 1983). Generally these birds departed between 6:00 and 8:00 A.M., flying "high and due south until out of binocular view."

My experience in tracking the first spring migrant hummingbirds entering New Mexico via Las Cruces, New Mexico, along the Rio Grande River, suggests that a cold snap sends early migrants retreating south. This behavior, advancing a notch at a time, has led me to suspect some early migrants advance northward no more than half the limit of their energy reserves. If a new food source isn't located, or if the weather turns cold, the birds seem to about-face and return to the safety of a known food source. Contributors to this tracking information live in Las Cruces, Truth or Consequences, Socorro, Albuquerque, Bernalillo, Santa Fe, Taos, and Questa, all in New Mexico.

Between June and August most hummingbirds begin moving south, toward their wintering grounds in the Caribbean Islands, Mexico, and Central America. Fall migration offers the second best opportunity to attract hummingbirds. Almost certainly the birds will linger where they find blossoms, leftover insects, or feeders. Where one hummingbird pauses, others usually gather, apparently sensing that a fellow has found food. Although fall migrants don't stay as long as spring arrivals, species numbers tend to increase.

There hasn't been much information on how high above ground level the birds fly when they migrate. In quest of data about the altitude at which hummingbirds fly, I asked a couple of hundred Albuquerque hot-air balloon pilots if they encountered hummingbirds as they floated aloft. Their answer was yes. Here are some balloonist reports of hummingbird sightings:

Frank Mezzancello: Hummingbird looked balloon over March 1990 at 200 feet.

Ken Fisher: Hummingbird investigated balloon at 200 feet.

Marsha Starr: Hummingbird investigated fluorescent orange surveyor's tape attached to crown line at "somewhere between 200 and 500 feet."

Beth Wheeler: Hummingbird poked up and down sides of [red] balloon. Altimeter read 200 feet above ground level.

The idea of visits from hummingbirds while floating through the air has appealed to many balloonists. Some now tie orange surveyor's tape on crown lines and gondolas in hope of enticing the birds to come up for a visit. Jay Mason, a commercial balloon operator in Albuquerque, was so intrigued he hung a feeder on his balloon in addition to tying bits of tape. Since New Mexico has thirteen species of hummingbirds plus more balloons than any place on the globe, in time we should have additional hummingbird altitude reports. These reports may answer not only the question how high do they fly but also how far do they see colors. There are other observations of how high these birds fly during migration.

Jesse Grantham of the National Audubon Society told me that the highest he saw migrating Ruby-throated hummingbirds passing Hawk Mountain in Pennsylvania was "around three hundred feet" (above ground level). Grantham also notes that it is common to see migrating Ruby-throats in the Texas coastal bend area following the shoreline "only a few feet high." In that same area, shrimp boat crewmen report they occasionally see Ruby-throated hummingbirds skim waves above Gulf of Mexico waters as far as 60 miles at sea. Seamen note that they also see sparrows and other land birds that far from land. Those observations lead me to suspect that sightings of land birds at sea result from birds being blown off course. (As a meteorologist I know the coastal bend of Texas to be one of the windiest areas in the U.S. Therefore, it would be relatively easy for a bird as small as a hummingbird to be accidentally blown miles out to sea.) Shrimp boat crewmen I talked with in the Rockport-Fulton area say when they see hummers at sea, the little birds invariably appear exhausted. Some boat operators hang hummingbird feeders on their craft to accommodate these tired travelers. And crewmen on off-shore drilling rigs as far as 200 miles out into the Gulf of Mexico report that once in a while a tired hummingbird perches on their drilling platform. (Hummingbird feeders on off shore drilling rigs would not only be good for hummingbirds, they might also prove to be good public relations for an environmentally sensitive oil company. Resulting PR would only be valid if the feeders were maintained after the media was gone.)

In western Mexico, fishermen in villages along Highway 200 north of Puerto Vallarta told me of seeing wave skimming hummers miles from land. My guess is these birds were enroute to and from islands 50 to 75 miles off the mainland.

There are a couple of reasons hummingbirds aren't likely to fly much higher above ground than balloon pilots and ground observers have thus far noted: (1) thinner air at higher altitudes requires more energy to maintain flight and (2) prey birds such as sparrow hawks, kites, and falcons could snag higher flying hummers out of the air. Hummingbird remains have been found in the stomach of a pigeon hawk (Lowery 1938), and a hummingbird was caught by a sparrow-hawk (Mayr 1966).

Incidentally, only a couple of hummingbirds hum while flying cross-country. One is the Broad-tailed. The buzz of passing Broad-tails is often heard before the birds are seen. The bird's flight sound, produced by adult males only, is caused by a slot at the tapered tip of the tenth primary wing feather (Miller & Inouye 1983). Wind rushing through these slots creates a noise similar to a cricket singing continuously, with no variation in tone. The tone is pitched at 6 khz, musically about F sharp. Rufous hummingbirds buzz, but to a lesser degree than Broad-tails. All other hummers fly silently cross-country, humming only while hovering or displaying at rivals.

Average speed of a migrating hummingbird is 25–30 mph, in still air. A tail wind could easily double that. Migrating bald eagles I have monitored make major moves only when tail winds prevail. I've also noted that migrating monarch butterflies perch when winds are unfavorable, and flutter on when the breeze shifts to a tail wind, north behind a cold front blowing toward their wintering grounds near El Rosario and Chincua, Mexico. As noted earlier, the first spring hummingbirds arrive in Albuquerque on a day when the wind blows from a general southern direction, from Mexico. Additionally, Mississippi kites invariably leave the Texas Panhandle and go south on the north winds behind a cold front. Jesse Grantham notes that Ruby-throats migrating through the coastal bend area of Texas tend to pause when winds are unfavorable, then proceed when tail winds prevail. A radar study of migrating bird flocks indicates that birds understand the effects wind patterns have on their cross-country flights (Bellrose & Graber 1967). Other geographical and meteorological features exist that may also influence hummingbird migration.

In the Americas, major mountain chains and rivers are oriented north and south, corresponding to bird migration routes. A theory suggests birds key on these (and other) topographic features, called guiding lines (Thompson 1960). The combination of prevailing winds and North American mountain ranges apparently provides not only navigational guidance, but also saves energy for many airborne creatures, including hummers. The Rockies have a greater variety of hummers than either the east coast's Appalachians, or the west coast's Sierra Nevadas. This suggests the Rockies have a special appeal to hummingbirds.

The Rocky Mountains enter the United States from Mexico via southwestern New Mexico's bootheel. At that point, a continuous ridge of summits and crests that is higher than neighboring terrain twists and turns northward. This ridge, known as the Continental Divide, splits the nation's east and west watersheds. The divide snakes 3,100 miles through the United States, roaming through New Mexico, Colorado, Wyoming and Montana before entering British Columbia, Canada. Several features unique to the divide make it attractive to hummingbirds.

Because the Divide rises higher in altitude than neighboring mountains, it automatically catches more precipitation, including snow, than lower elevations. In spring, more snowmelt translates into a more abundant, more dependable supply of flowers and insects, not only along the divide, but also along its slopes and within its valleys. Since flowers and insects attract hummingbirds, it's logical this "flower highway" is a magnet for hummers in spring. Another feature of the divide is especially attractive to migrating hummers (and other birds as well).

Winds blowing against mountains are deflected upward. A bird flying no higher than a couple of hundred feet in this buoyant updraft is effectively flying downhill, while maintaining a level altitude above the ground. For northbound birds, the more southerly the wind, the more a tail wind component would be added to the updraft factor, and vice versa for southbound birds. Then, in late summer, a meteorological event happens that further enhances the divide as a hummingbird haven.

In the last days of June and the first days of July the southwest's monsoon rains begin. Through July and August, these rains fall from thunderstorms generated over mountains. The daily afternoon formation of these storms is so consistent, one can nearly set one's watch by them. The Continental Divide again catches more precipitation than neighboring lower grounds. The monsoon rains bring forth a new flower crop that blooms through late summer and into September and October. These flowers offer favorable fall hummingbird migration conditions. Adult and young hummingbirds cruising toward winter-

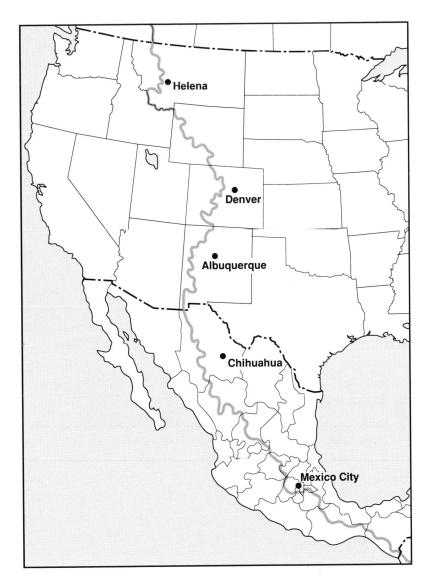

Map of Continental Divide.

ing grounds in Mexico forage along the flower highway that served nectar, insects, and updraft winds in the spring. Further evidence that the divide is a hummingbird flyway comes from this: one quarter of all recorded trips longer than 400 miles made by banded hummers have points of origin and recapture along the Continental Divide (personal communication with Office of Migratory Bird Management, 1991).

After I explained my Continental Divide observations to Dr. Bill Calder, he banded hummingbirds at four locations near the divide in New Mexico. In ten days in August 1991, Bill and his wife captured, banded, and released 964 hummingbirds that included five species (230 were banded in a single day). At a backyard location near Silver City, New Mexico, Bill estimated the total population at between 1,100 and 1,300 hummers. By contrast in Ramsey Canyon, Arizona, a total of 215 hummingbirds were banded during the entire year of 1991. Calder rated the Continental Divide banding experience as his most productive in twenty-one years of chasing hummers throughout the southwest and Mexico. Prior to that August banding, Calder's lifetime total of banded hummingbirds was just over 7,000. He is the world's leader in hummingbird banding.

As further evidence that hummingbird populations are large along the divide, consider that the important hummingbird banding station, the Rocky Mountain Biological Laboratory near Gothic, Colorado, is located near the Continental Divide. And along the divide in Costa Rica, the Monteverde Cloud Forest is also apparently a prime hummingbird area. I'm told by master bander Nancy Newfield of Metairie, Louisiana, that she sees more species of hummingbirds (ten to twelve) in the Monteverde area than other places she visits in Central and South America.

In the United States, a Continental Divide hiking trail, twenty-three years in the making so far, is being cleared across New Mexico, Colorado, Wyoming, and Montana. Trail workers and hikers say they hear or see hummingbirds many times along the trail, especially in spring and fall. Officials forecast completion of the 790-mile New Mexico section by the mid-1990s.

Smaller mountain chains in the southwest are also utilized by hummingbirds; however, I find those lower mountains have smaller numbers of hummingbirds than the divide's. East and west coast mountain ranges are used by hummingbirds in the same manner as the Rocky Mountains. The difference in numbers of species could be due to the fact that the Rockies serve as a main guiding line from Mexico, where many hummingbird species winter. In addition to what I have come to call the "mountain-hummingbird connection," an air mass peculiar to the United States may explain why the Rufous humming-bird migrates over more territory than any other North American hummingbird.

The peak of a dome of high pressure air centered in the western U.S. tends to persist over Utah. This dome, known as the Great Basin High, generally sprawls over most of the western part of the country like a giant inverted mixing bowl. The system periodically circulates winds on the dome's edge up from Mexico into southern California. Winds continue clockwise around the high through Nevada, Oregon, and Washington, curving right into Montana. Winds of the "average"-sized Great Basin High continue curving right, looping south from Montana through Wyoming, Colorado, and New Mexico. These winds then curve westward across Arizona to complete their loop in southern California. This circulation forms a loop that matches known migration patterns of some western hummingbirds, including the Rufous (Phillips 1975).

Occasionally an average Great Basin High builds enough to be-come a "super high." A super high's asymmetric clockwise circula-tion, with an eccentric center over or near Utah, is large enough to encompass the entire U.S. and most of Canada. Hummingbird sight-ings, especially the Rufous, parallel the clockwise circulation of these super high pressure systems (Conway & Drennan 1979).

Winds from a super high from western Alaska and western Canada expand to form the top of an oval across the northern states and Canada, as far east as Newfoundland and Maine. With distance, this massive, blue-sky weather system's winds continue curving right, flowing down the east coast as far as the Bahamas and Florida. Con-tinuing to curve right, the winds bend cross the southern states from Florida to southern California, where they are known as Santa Anna winds. Air moving around a super Great Basin High completes its loop by curving up the west coast through California toward Ore-gon, Washington, Canada, and so on. A super Great Basin High gives weathermen little to talk about, because it propagates blue skies from coast to coast and border to border. At times a weakening high is interrupted by cold fronts or other systems, but invariably the high rebuilds in time, sometimes persisting from four to eight days. A hummingbird riding the wind could make between 1,200 and 2,400 miles during the life of one super Great Basin High, including pauses to feed.

In late winter, Rufous and other hummingbird movements have

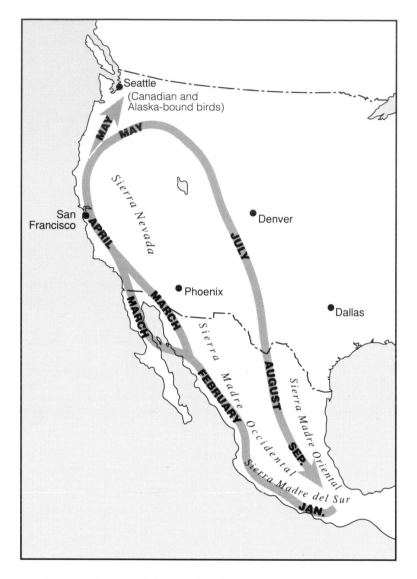

Apparent migrations of adult male S. rufus that breed in Montana and Idaho.

been plotted northward from Mexican wintering grounds into southern California. Their flight path matches an average Great Basin High's wind field. As summer progresses many, along with a few Calliope, apparently follow the high's circulation from Washington across Montana and then south through the mountain states of Wyoming, Colorado, and New Mexico (Phillips 1975). However, a few Rufous, Black-chins, and Calliope apparently ride a super Great Basin High across Canada to Newfoundland and Maine, then southward along the eastern seaboard from Maine to Florida and the Bahamas. In late summer and early fall, these birds move through the southern United States, apparently on their way back to winter in Mexico. That these migrations may be more than a fluke is indicated by a female Rufous that has shown up at the same feeder in Atlanta three consecutive years. Based on Bill Calder's banding experience, which indicates individual hummingbirds tend to fly precisely the same route each year, it is probably safe to assume the Atlanta bird is the same bird. In Calder's words on the proclivity of hummingbirds to stick to a learned route, "Juveniles learn well on their first solo migration flight, apparently born to realize that if it works, don't try something else [next year] that might not." Additionally, in the winter of 1990–1991 a male Rufous remained on the Palos Verdes peninsula near Los Angeles; a young male Rufous wintered in the Surry, Maine area, accepting the hospitality of Donna Robinson's greenhouse; several Rufous hummingbirds spent the winter in Georgia and Alabama; and a couple of Rufous wintered in Tucson. Each of these overwintering birds were on the perimeter of a super Great Basin High's circulation. And in the five years before and including 1991, hummingbird banders Bob and Martha Sargent of Trussville, Alabama, have recorded 58 Rufous, 35 Black-chinned, 2 Calliope, and an Allen's, distributed across Georgia, Alabama, Tennessee, Mississippi, and Florida. All of these western birds could have ridden a super Great Basin's continental merry-go-round. (Rufous hummingbirds have been reported in 47 of America's 49 North American states.)

Rufous hummers that take advantage of both east and west coast mountain upslope winds, plus super Great Basin High winds, may be covering more territory than any U.S. hummingbird. If time proves a few Rufous are riding the perimeter of a super Great Basin High, with time out to breed plus a side trip deep into Mexico, this smallest of all birds is traveling a migration route measuring between 11,000 and 11,500 miles. The Arctic tern is currently affirmed as the world's champion long-distance traveler. Banding records have proven this tern travels an 11,000-mile route that is nearly pole to pole (Austin

1928). When we consider that Arctic tern wings span 33 inches, this possible flight of Rufous hummingbirds, weighing little more than a penny, is impressive.

Additional banded hummingbird recoveries will be needed to determine if a Rufous displaces the Arctic tern from title of "World Champion Distance Traveler of the Bird World." At this point, only one banded hummingbird (a Black-chinned) has been verified on both its wintering grounds in Mexico and its summer breeding grounds in the United States. Part of the reason is that to date, only 77,000 hummingbirds have been banded, out of a total of 50,309,044 bird bandings, through the spring of 1992 (personal communication with Bird Banding Laboratory).

Banded hummingbird recoveries are scarce. To date, only 40 banded hummingbirds (10 species) have been recovered away from their banding site since hummingbird banding began in Massachusetts in 1932 (personal communication with Bird Banding Laboratory). One reason for so few recoveries is because there are only thirty-nine active hummingbird banders in the United States. And, finding a banded hummingbird that died enroute is difficult compared to finding a dead eagle or goose. (If you find a banded bird of any kind, you add to the store of bird migration knowledge by reporting its number to The Bird Banding Laboratory, Laurel, Maryland, 20708–9619). The longest hummingbird flights documented to date are:

Rufous, 1,733 miles (2,773 km) near Clark, Colorado, to Yes Bay, Alaska

Rufous, 1,414 miles (2,262 km) from Ramsey Canyon, Arizona, to near Mt. Saint Helens, Washington

Rufous, 1,090 miles (1,744 km) from Gothic, Colorado, to an island east of Nanaimo, Vancouver Island, Canada

Rufous, 1,030 miles (1,648 km) from Gothic, Colorado, to the Lumi Reservation west of Bellingham, Washington

Black-chinned, 930 miles (1,488 km) from southeast Arizona to near Manzanillo, Mexico

Calliope, 773 miles (1,237 km) from Libby, Montana, to Gothic, Colorado (Banding and recovery points are near Continental Divide mountains.)

Rufous, 747 miles (1,195 km) from Swan Lake, Montana, to Gothic, Colorado (Banding and recapture points are near the Continental Divide. Trip was accomplished in a record fifteen days, suggesting the bird's flight may have paralleled the divide.)

Ruby-throated, 719 miles (1,150 km) from Grove, Oklahoma, to

Carlton, Minnesota

Rufous, 644 miles (1,039 km) from California to Oregon

Ruby-throated, 618 miles (989 km) from Somerset, Pennsylvania, to Quebec, Canada

Rufous, 562 miles (899 km) from Pensacola, Florida, to Springfield, Missouri.

Allen's, 504 miles (806 km) from California to Arizona

Ruby-throated, 497 miles (795 km) from south of Grove, Oklahoma, to Kerrville, Texas

Allen's, 482 miles (771 km) from San Francisco, California, to San Diego, California

Calliope, 434 miles (694 km) from the San Bernardino Mountains, California, to Sonoita, Arizona

Rufous, 422 miles (675 km) from near Silver City, New Mexico, to Gothic, Colorado (Banding and recovery points are near the Continental Divide.)

If evidence verifies that a few Rufous do make the 11,000–11,500 mile journey, preliminary banding records (Calder 1987) suggest it would take a year for the birds to complete a migratory circuit along a super Great Basin High route. Rufous hummingbirds that fly the long route would be essentially "permanent transients," traveling most of their lives.

Some believe the Rufous' apparent expansion across the U.S., Canada, and the Bahamas is due in part to feeders and flower plantings along the path of super Great Basin High tail winds. However, records of Rufous hummingbirds appearing along the eastern seaboard date back to 1909 (Conway & Drennan 1979), well before the development of hummingbird feeders (True 1993). For more information about the Rufous, refer to the photo/biographical section.

An extensive study on Rufous migration will be needed to prove or disprove this theory. For now, however, it seems logical to assume that natural selection might support birds recognizing and responding to favorable wind patterns, because beneficial winds reduce energy consumption and flight time (Hassler et al. 1963). When I hear of a hummingbird that "strayed off course," I suspect the little rascal was simply riding a tail wind and headed somewhere on purpose. A super Great Basin High's circulation might explain observations of Ruby-throats, normally eastern birds, along the west coast. These "strays" could have hopped on super Great Basin High winds in eastern or southeastern states and ridden the breeze westward to California. Other Ruby-throats may migrate on a different wind.

Fall migration for eastern hummingbirds coincides with the peak of the gulf states' hurricane season. Tail winds generated by a distant hurricane's outer winds flow toward Cuba and Mexico. These tail-winds might influence Ruby-throat fall migration departure times. Certainly, such a wind would increase the feasibility of a gulf crossing flight to Mexico. Then in spring, for a return to the states, birds may ride tail winds blowing from Cuba and Mexico back toward the United States. These spring winds are spawned by what is known as the Bermuda High.

Other western hummingbirds that seem to stray off their normal paths may have hopped onto tail winds of cold fronts moving from northwest toward southeast. These fronts, not related to Great Basin Highs, sweep roughly from Washington, Oregon, and California on a straightforward east-to-southeast run. These cold frontal movements could collect western hummers—Allen's, Anna's, Blue-throated, Magnificent, Lucifer, Broad-billed, Calliope, etc.— and concentrate them where land ends, such as Texas and Louisiana coastal areas, and to a lesser degree, eastern Gulf Coast states.

During spring or fall migration, if passing birds fail to stay in your yard, it is still a good idea to leave a feeder up. Traveling birds may note its location and stop next season.

Observations on Hummingbird Wintering in Mexico

Generally, Mexican attitudes toward environmental conservation are positive, especially among individuals. For example, when I was looking for Lucifer hummingbirds to film, I paused in the small, dirt-street village of La Barranca, south of Highway 49 and a few miles west of San Luis Potosi. Resistance from La Barranca people toward my inquiry about hummingbirds was obvious, and puzzling. It wasn't until I realized the people feared I wanted to capture, and possibly haul off hummingbirds that I recognized the problem. As soon as I assured them I wanted only to photograph the birds, and would neither capture nor touch them, their attitude changed from semi-hostile to friendly and cooperative. One man even volunteered to take me to an old nest. I found their protectiveness toward wildlife refreshing. (Later, I discovered street vendors selling caged hummingbirds in larger towns, such as Cuernavaca, Morelia. The fact that outsiders were capturing hummingbirds could explain the villagers' initial coolness toward me when I asked about the birds.)

Near the town of Chamala, on a mountain dirt road west of Cuernavaca, I asked a local motorcycle policeman, who was working on his machine with friends beside the road, about hummingbirds. The man lamented the loss of an area in the valley, where hummingbirds had been numerous. He explained that a couple of years ago the valley's river was dammed to form a lake, "Laguna Tempoala" (spelling may not be exact). He said that since lake Tempoala flooded the valley, their hummingbirds had disappeared.

Major losses of wildlife habitat in Mexico south of Brownsville, Texas are a threat to hummers. Mexico's northeast coast is undergoing changes that especially touch Buff-bellied hummingbirds. Coastal lands are being cleared of natural vegetation for planting of commercial crops. (Clearing and replanting are also prevalent along Texas' south coast). Natural vegetation held many nectar-producing flowers that Buff-bellied hummingbirds depended upon year round. (Other hummers, especially the Ruby-throated, fed from these flowers during migrations.) It is possible this habitat loss is behind the increase in Buff-bellied sightings in Texas, Louisiana, Alabama, Georgia, and Florida.

In Mexico's national forests, government sponsored billboards with a Monarch butterfly logo remind that it is illegal to disturb animals, plants, and/or minerals. The sign's theme is good for hummingbirds. However, trucks loaded with logs frequently groan past the signs on their way out of the forests.

Logging in Mexico's national forests is conducted under concessions granted by the government. Currently, logging operations destroy 3 percent of Mexico's forests each year. And in 1991 the Mexican legislature was tinkering with Article 27, which since the 1910–1917 revolution, has guaranteed the integrity of *ejido* communal lands to peasant farmers (*campesinos*). The government's proposal was to "confiscate" communal lands from rural "owners" and sell that land to commercial timber and mining interests. David Luhnow, a reporter in Mexico City, wrote: "Every year, around 500,000 hectares of Mexican forest fall to the ax of commercial development. As the trees die, so do Mexico's plant and animal species, at a rate of one per day. Recent proposed changes in the *ejido* communal farm system will either save Mexico's beleaguered forests, or finish them off" (*The News* 1991a). The death of millions of Monarch butterflys in the state of Michoacan, Mexico, may portend the fate of some species of hummingbirds. Ecologist Humero Ardjis noted a forest used by Monarchs became a butterfly graveyard after deforestation (*Albuquerque Tribune* 1992).

Obviously, changes affecting peasant land ownership in Mexico would most likely not bode well for hummingbirds. Opposition, however, to these proposed changes is strong. *Campesinos* have threatened to choke Mexico's capital by "blockading all major highways." The peasants also vow to oppose government sponsored land use changes by "blowing up bridges if we need to" (*The News* 1991b). Better news came from the Yucatan peninsula.

In Cancun (Ruby-throated, Rufous-tailed, and Buff-bellied country), a tourism megaproject was downsized because experts said it would have a negative impact on Nichupte Lagoon. At the same time, spokespeople for Grupo Ecologista del Maya (GEMA) said, "As much as we like this downsizing, many other ecological problems with the megaproject have yet to be resolved" (*The News* 1991c).

The following unusual hummingbird legend I got from Sr. Silverio Garcia Garcia on a dirt street in Leon Guzman, west of Torreon.

Garcia told of how young women in his home pueblo of Tamazula, Jalisco (south of Guadalajara), take the heart of a hummingbird and place it in the sun to dry. The dried hummingbird heart is pulverized into powder. A woman then secretly stirs a tiny portion of hummingbird heart dust into coffee she offers the man of her choice. The hummer heart potion is supposed to render the woman irresistibly attractive to the man. Garcia emphasized that the powdered hummer heart was a love potion, and not an aphrodisiac. This practice may have been carried into modern times from tales of native Indians who wore stuffed hummers in the belief that the amulet focused irresistible sexual attraction to the wearer.

After years of travel throughout Mexico I have seen only one hummingbird feeder maintained by a Mexican national. That feeder (American made) was at a small mansion in the modern, upscale village of Magdalena Petlacalco, D.F., overlooking Mexico City. On the other hand, many retired Americans and Canadians living in Mexico have feeders. Since I have never seen hummingbird feeders for sale in Mexico, I would guess the economy is the reason so little backyard feeding is done by Mexican citizens. The lowest priced American feeder I know of is $2.95. At the current exchange rate, that would approximately be 8800 Mexican pesos. Few Mexican people can afford that many pesos for an item such as a hummingbird feeder. Maybe it takes a sizable, economically robust middle class to afford hummingbird feeders.

Hummingbird Colors

Hummingbird colors are created by feathers with a grid structure, a grating effect that produces evenly scored lines, with both sides of the grid covered by a smooth membrane. Components of white light entering this feather structure are split (refracted) into separate colors. Different spacing of the grating in each species, as well as among individual feathers, determines which color wavelength will be refracted. (Refracted light produces colors in their purest form. Rainbow colors are produced by refracted light. Also, light from a diamond's facets is refracted.) Because of their unique feather design, hummingbirds have purer colors than most birds. In a way, they are small bits of flying rainbows. One way to enjoy this color show is to place feeders in cool morning or late evening sunlight to maximize the bird's colors. Then move the feeders into shade during hotter hours. With a little more effort, there is a way to provide the birds with shaded feeders all day, while you have a color show anytime, at the flip of a switch.

A halogen floodlamp approximates the sun's white light. By placing a feeder in permanent shade and lighting it with a halogen floodlamp (or a photo flood lamp), a kaleidoscope of colors can be mined from the birds' feather design. When hummers come to feed, and move about in the floodlight, their gorgets light up like neon signs. Colors twinkle from one rainbow shade to another, or blink "out", only to wink back "on" in tune with their aerial activity. Two lamps pointed toward a feeder at 90 degrees to each other and aimed down to at least a 20 degree angle maximizes this color show. In my view, lighting a feeder is a quantum leap toward increasing hummingbird enjoyment.

Positioning the lamp (and yourself) lower than the feeder will enhance your view of the bird's throat and undersides. Placing the lamp higher than the feeder will sparkle topside colors. Ten to fifteen minutes of show is generally satisfying, and heat buildup on feeders is nil. If you want longer light shows, lamps should be placed far enough from feeders so as not to warm their solution. An on-off switch provides before and after views. The difference is as dramatic as the difference between black-and-white and color television. This hummingbird light show is an "ah-ha" experience of a caliber both children and adults long remember.

A PAR38 CAP/FL outdoor halogen floodlamp is a good choice. Priced around $10.00, the lamp is available in wattages from 45 to 150. A fixture to hold the lamp costs under $3.00. I use two 45-watt lamps, mounted on camera tripods right and left of the feeder, three feet away, and angled 90 degrees to each other.

Because floodlighting highlights color facets you otherwise miss, halogen lamps are a useful tool for species identification. For example, near Sayre, in western Oklahoma, this system identified Ruby-throated hummingbirds that were not listed as being there. Observation time needed for identification was considerably shortened. The first Ruby-throated male that came to a lighted feeder was obvious. Halogen lighting not only saved time, it also revealed there was an overlapping of Ruby-throats and Black-chins in that area. More importantly, the lights hinted there might be crossbreeding between the species. As the birds danced in the light, some male Black-chins had traces of red Ruby-throat colors in their otherwise blue gorgets, and vice versa. Traces of colors in these possibly crossbred birds were so subtle, without lamps it is unlikely we would have seen those hues. (The *Bulletin of Oklahoma Ornithological Society* 2:14–15 presents evidence suggesting there may be a hybrid Black-chin-Ruby-throat.) However, if artificial lighting to enhance hummingbird colors sounds like too much work, or if such lights would consume more electrical energy than suits your lifestyle, simply place feeders where it is sometimes shady and sometimes sunny and let nature take its course. For another world of hummingbird colors, position yourself to look straight down on sunlit birds. Of course, hummingbird colors help nature take her course in getting male and female hummingbirds together.

Mating

Several days after the males arrive in the spring, females appear. Almost immediately the little hens are given a showboat courtship flight by the males. There is a study suggesting the enthusiasm of a male's amorous flight reflects his impression of the amount of available food (Tamm 1985). Apparently the mature male bird's hormones are pumped up when he finds plentiful food. In this condition, the little fellow puts on airshows that look as if they are designed to demonstrate to lady hummingbirds that he is well fed, healthy, virile, and worthy of her consideration.

People who have seen male hummingbirds performing aerial hijinks at mating time describe the event with a certain breathlessness. Invariably, these descriptions sound as if the little males were flying in other than a normal mode. New evidence indicates different flight patterns for courtship, and for defending territory. Both territory and courtship flight reflects a tactic employed by Spitfire 1 aircraft in the sky over England during the Battle of Britain in World War II.

At the Rocky Mountain Biological Laboratory near Gothic, Colorado, a team lead by Bill Calder rigged scales equipped with a perch. The scales were accurate to $\frac{1}{100}$ of a gram. The perch-scales weighed territory defending/courting male Broad-tails each time the birds landed. The team learned that territorial male hummingbirds fed lightly following each sortie to chase an intruder. Scale readings showed that the weight of these hummers increased only 1–2 percent during the day. Then, at dusk, when rival birds had perched for the night and territory defense was no longer necessary, these males gorged their weights up by as much as 34–40 percent in a few feedings (Calder 1991). During this period the hummingbird hens fed normally and therefore less frequently than their mates. There was method in the male Broad-tail's eating habits.

By keeping themselves light, these territory defending/courtship flying hummingbirds accelerated faster and were more maneuverable in aerial battles against intruders. British aircraft engineers who designed the Spitfire 1 fighter plane used this same "keep 'em light" tactic.

The 1939 Spitfire 1 carried 85 gallons of fuel . . . just enough for one combat patrol of an hour and a half, including fifteen minutes of dogfight time. Because the aircraft was designed to fight over home territory, on combat missions with a radius of no more than 197 miles, the craft didn't need "extra" fuel. Without the burdensome weight of surplus fuel, which weighs six pounds per gallon, the Spitfire 1 accelerated faster, climbed quicker, and was more nimble during aerial combat. With its lightweight advantage, the aircraft trounced heavier invaders who outnumbered it four to one. (The 1944 MkXVI Spitfires that chased enemy aircraft across Europe tripled fuel loadings to 255 gallons.)

Lightness also equals aerial superiority for hummingbirds. On sorties against intruders, or in display flights for female attention, these lightly fueled male hot rod hummers outfly rivals. Less wonder that these flights are spectacular. Calder's findings that the males keep themselves light during working hours reinforces my feeling there is a reason for everything in nature.

In courtship, the male flies a yo-yo pattern of high-speed dives that look like 200 mph but in reality top at 64 mph, with an average of 40 through his circuit (Pearson 1960). Courtship flights of each species are slightly different, which may be nature's way of reducing cross-breeding. With variations, the male's flight consists of buzzing back and forth in a pendulum swing in front of his intended. This part of his show is done facing the sun, which enhances his gorget colors. Apparently males add the side to side pendulum swing to make certain the sun's rays intercept that narrow angle which maximizes gorget iridescence. In an additional attempt to help the sun catch their colors, some males, such as the Lucifer and Costa's, fluff out their gorgets during their pendulum swings. On cloudy days the male seems indifferent to the direction he faces. The male bird's flight includes zooms upward 20–50 feet, into a position for repeating his dive, and a screeching halt in front of the hen for a repeat of his pendulum shuttle.

Through his courtship flight, the male is probably signaling to the female that he deserves to be chosen because he is in command of a food source rich enough for her to raise a family. As proof the little male's demonstration is on track, a study in Arizona and New Mexico showed that areas containing greater quantities and more predictable nectar supplies tended to have more nests (Baltosser 1989). Clearly, for hummingbirds to nest in your area, it is important to have a feeder filled and available before the first male arrives in spring. It is also important that when the first bird arrives, additional feeders be offered, especially one for the female. Her feeder should be away from concentrated hummingbird traffic. In effect, this feeder becomes hers, and helps to further convince her the area contains food enough to raise young. This feeder should be equipped with a perch to accommodate the female when she is heavy with eggs. (Weight increase from eggs is 10–20 percent. Her egg carrying weight would determine the size of wings necessary to support that weight, and may be the reason most female hummingbirds are slightly larger, with bigger wings, than males.) Her feeder should have more than one port, to make it easier for her to teach young birds how to feed themselves. After I located a feeder especially for a female Black-chinned which had laid her eggs, that little hen became a tiger around her feeder, aggressive enough to drive away other hummingbirds, including males.

Most hummingbirds that breed in the United States and Canada have little or no song. Possibly the male's flashy flight, combined with his flashy colors, supplants singing as a way to let other males as well as females know of his presence. (Laurel Kelley of Patzcuaro, Michoacan, Mexico, says the reason hummers hum is because they don't know the words.)

Although North American hummingbirds, except for Anna's, Berylline, and Costa's, are considered to be without song, the birds punctuate mating flights with feeble squeaks. Some observers believe hummingbirds may sing a song pitched beyond detection by human ears . . . a song heard only by other hummers. Eagles have no song either, and I find it interesting that male eagles also perform yo-yo aerial maneuvers at mating time. The eagle's display flight pattern, from ground level up to 600–700 feet, is almost identical to the hummingbird's. The eagle's flight, too, is marked by feeble little squawks. My research indicates that a golden eagle can eat as much as 2¼ pounds at one feeding, or 25–30 percent of its weight, which leads me to wonder if the male eagle eats lightly during his month-long courtship.

After the hummingbird males have performed their flashy flights, it is generally believed the birds mate. Following are eleven accounts of hummingbird matings.

The first account I found was about the Calliope. L. E. Wyman states: "[the male Calliope] darted down again in a long, narrow, vertical ellipse that flattened where it touched the hill side. As he passed the female she fluttered and swung head downward on her perch. The male alighted above her, with vibrating wings, and coition took place in this position" (Wyman 1920).

The second hummingbird mating account I found was by G. D. Sprot: "On two occasions, in May 1925 and 1926, I witnessed what I believe to be the actual mating of the birds. After one or two towering flights by the male [Rufous], the female rose from her perch and the male immediately closed with her. Then over a distance of some ten or twelve feet, and horizontally, they swung together backwards and forwards through the air, just as one often sees insects so doing. The regular swinging hum of the wings is hard to describe but is just what one might expect. So fast is this swinging flight, and so close was I, not over four or five feet away in one instance, that I was totally unable to see the birds except as a blurred streak of color. As the flight ceased I saw them separate, and in one instance the female fell to the ground, but later regained her perch, while the male continued his towering flights" (Sprot 1925–26).

Leroy W. Arnold states his observation of mating Anna's. "When first observed, the birds were playfully chasing each other about and suddenly swooped down to within about eighteen inches of the ground where the leading bird, which proved to be the female, stopped and faced about. The male approached and the mating was consummated in the air, the birds breast to breast and with the male somewhat under the female. The male then settled down to the ground for a few moments, fanning out his tail and pointing his beak upward, while the female flew to a nearby perch. After a short rest, the male rose and flew after the female who returned to her former position and mating again took place as before" (Arnold 1930).

The next mating account I located was of Allen's hummingbirds in San Francisco. It simply stated that "the birds copulated in mid-air" (Orr 1939).

Another mating account was by Frank Bené of Phoenix: "On April 4 a male (Black-chinned) courted and copulated with a female on the ground across the fence near the grape arbor" (Bené 1942:429).

On June 2, 1945, Louise Hering observed Broad-tailed humming-bird mating in a pine forest about fifteen miles northeast of Colorado Springs, Colorado. In Louise's words, "The female remained perched on a willow branch and the male alighted over her. After copulation, she shook her feathers and preened for several minutes before flying away" (Hering 1945).

Betty Trousdale observed Anna's hummingbirds mating in Oakland, California, August 30, 1953, at about 2:00 P.M. "Suddenly the female flew from the oak tree and perched on another clothesline over our heads. Instantly the male left his perch to hover over and then mount the female. During the few seconds of copulation the male's wings fluttered rapidly, while the female remained perched. Immediately after copulation, the female returned to the oak tree and the male to his perch on the clothesline" (Trousdale 1954).

In 1964 observers saw Costa's mate. The male and female were perched on open mesquite twigs in Arizona when the male launched and approached the female from the front. The male made short darting flights toward her from various angles within an arc of about 90 degrees. He then mounted her while she was perched, disengaged and flew off, and again darted at her from the front. The two then flew off, one in close pursuit of the other (Miller 1964).

The following Black-chinned mating observation is by Joanne Phillips of Albuquerque, New Mexico. In 1975 Joanne watched a male perform his high-stepping courtship flight in front of a little hen. Joanne remembers it was about 8:00 in the morning, sometime in May. "The hen (a Black-chinned) was perched in outer branches of a cottonwood. The female watched the male's courtship flight a moment, then flew to the lower part of the tree and perched on a bare branch. The male continued yo-yos for ten or fifteen seconds, then zipped to the female."

Joanne describes the male Black-chinned's physical contact with the female as more of a "quick touch and go" on her back, rather than a landing. Joanne finished her account by noting that, "Almost immediately the female flew one way, while he flew another." We have not determined if this is the way Black-chins copulate or if what Joanne saw was only a preliminary encounter.

Mating

In 1985 Kenneth and Effie Evans observed Ruby-throated hummingbirds mating in Branson, Missouri. "May 14, 1985, while washing breakfast dishes, we observed Ruby-throated hummingbirds copulating on the top branch of an American holly bush five to six feet from our window. The female was hanging upside down from the holly's branch, head and breast below the branch and tail above. The male hovered above, and was in contact with her. She hung motionless and appeared to be mesmerized. At the act's completion the male flew to an adjoining branch in the holly. The hen remained suspended, upside down. After a brief moment the male returned to her and they mated again. This mating lasted a minute or two."

The Evanses continue, "After mating the hen righted herself, roused, shook out her feathers, and flew to a feeder at our kitchen window. The hen landed on one of the feeder's perchs. The port in front of the perch was closed off, therefore the birds seldom approached it. Almost as soon as she was on the feeder's perch he grabbed her bill with his and remounted her. Her tongue became visible, and she again seemed mesmerized. Her head and breast rotated forward, her tail feathers went up and she was again suspended upside down. The male hovered over her, moving from side to side. Then, either her tail feathers separated or he separated them, and they copulated again. The birds repeatedly mated in this manner over a time span of twenty to thirty minutes. During this series she remained upside down, with her eyes closed, as though she was lifeless."

During the spring of 1986 in Cedaredge, Colorado, Dave Nunn saw what he believes were Broad-tailed hummingbirds mating on the wing. Nunn said the male appeared to ride the female's back on the downswing of a pendulum dive that is part of the bird's courtship ritual. At the bottom of the pendulum, after the birds had began the upside, they separated. Nunn said he saw this sequence occur on different days a couple of times during that spring.

From these hummingbird mating accounts, note that generally no species is described as mating like another. Calliope apparently mate rather conventionally; Rufous are observed to mate like flying mating insects, possibly such as dragonflies; Anna's are described as mating breast to breast; Black-chins seem to mate within a fleeting instant; Ruby-throats were observed making a production of mating; and Broad-tails may mate in flight, piggy-back style. From these accounts, and from observations that the males of each hummingbird species seem to perform slightly different courtship flights, I'm led to speculate that different hummingbird species mate differently. That would parallel the mating behavior of golden eagles compared with bald eagles. The former mate on the ground, the latter on the wing as high as 5,000 feet in the air. These differing mating methods of similar species may be nature's attempt to reduce the chance of crossbreeding.

After fertilization, there is evidence the female allows the male in her territory for several days. There is evidence the two perch near each other, or even together for several days following mating. I have seen a Black-chinned pair come to a feeder and perch at the same time during nest building and around the time of egg laying. However, that closeness apparently ends and the hummingbird hens raise their chicks alone. Bené observes, "The fact that the entire burden of caring for the young falls on the female hummer makes it all the more imperative that she choose a nest site as close as possible to abundant food. She cannot afford to depend on a haphazard food supply nor undertake long excursions in quest of it."

After mating, the males pursue, and often mate with, other hens. As noted earlier, females live an average of three-and-a-half years while males live an average of only two-and-a-half. Under that imbalance, polygamous males seem a natural solution to maintaining hummingbird populations.

A proposed theory for why male hummingbirds don't stay around to help brood and raise the young is that, with his brighter colors, a male might attract predators to a nest. However, biologists at the University of New Mexico point out that the brightly colored male Grosbeak helps his hen with egg incubation, and after hatch, helps rear the young. Apparently his staying around the nest doesn't attract Grosbeak predators. These biologists suggest that the female hummingbird ignores the male after mating because a hen hummingbird needs no help in incubating eggs or rearing young. She can brood eggs alone for the 14 days of incubation (Black-chinned), and she can provide food enough to raise the young alone, which takes an additional three-and-a-half weeks. In that light it may be inaccurate to claim the male hummingbird "goes his way" after mating. In his hummingbird brain the male may sense there is no need for him to remain near the hen after fertilization. At the same time, her brain may realize there aren't enough males to go around, therefore she has no choice but to be a single parent.

By contrast, eagles mate for life, are monogamous, and copulate throughout the six months of courtship, egg incubation, and young rearing. A probable reason for eagles mating for life is that eagle hens need mates to help brood eggs through forty-one days of incubation, plus help through eleven weeks of catching game to feed their nestling(s). With the male eagle involved in rearing young, he is in a position to protect his gene investment, and remains monogamous. But the male hummingbird is left to go his way, and therefore denied the opportunity to protect his gene investment in one hen. His mating with others may be male hummingbird strategy for insuring his lineage. Regardless, after mating, the hummingbird hen goes about the business of building a nest.

Nesting

Hummingbird nests are about the size of half an English walnut shell. Exquisitely tiny and ingeniously camouflaged, a hummingbird nest is difficult to spot. The philosophic nature writer John Burroughs was so impressed with a hummingbird nest he regarded finding one "an event to date from."

My appreciation for the uniqueness of hummingbird nests began when I filmed a nesting Black-chinned hen. At the nest's beginning,

Black-chinned nest egg.

the female landed in the diamond-shaped openings of my chain link fence. There she carefully chose strands of spider webbing that had become caught on the fence. From the fence, she flew with the webbing flowing from her beak. Her trip to a tree was a slow-motion, semi-hovering flight suggesting she was directing downwash from her wings in a way that prevented the spider silks from entangling. Her spider-web flight was a slow, laborious forward climb. That the flight took place in calm air caused me to suspect she specifically chose those conditions to make a spider-web cargo flight. However, reproductive biology being as relentless as it is, I suspect if the day had been windy when her time was near, she would still collect and carry spider webbing. I have photographs of females with spider webbing entangling their tail feathers during a period of several windy days that matched nest-building time. (I find it interesting that the "umbrella" spider that released the silk and rode the air on a parachute strand contributed nest-building material to a bird that may one day eat the spider's eggs or young, or even the spider itself.)

The female hummingbird's tree of choice for her nest was a fruitless mulberry that also held a dove nest. Her tree was closely sheltered by another tree. Of most nests I've seen, this arrangement is common.

Compared with the loose stick arrangement of the dove nest, the hummingbird nest was a classy, well-engineered work of art. The nest was 6 feet above the ground, in the tree's lowest limbs. The limb she had chosen was a couple of inches in diameter. The second day into the nest's construction I heard robins raising a ruckus, suggesting maybe a cat was about. When I went outside to investigate, a roadrunner sailed from the tree, apparently startled by me. The mother dove was on the ground doing her broken wing act. Baby dove, or baby hummingbird, would serve as a roadrunner snack.

The hummingbird abandoned that nest site and began construction in a neighboring fruitless mulberry. This time she chose a mid-level branch 18 feet high, and she built far out near the branch's end, where it had a diameter of less than an inch. Construction of the second nest continued eight days, and she took some material from her first nest and used it again.

A few days after I saw the hummer's spider-web flight, the bird hovered on all sides of a wisp of floating cottonwood seed tuft, again in calm air. It appeared she was deciding from which angle to grasp the floating "cotton." After the bird drifted with the tuft a few seconds she plucked it out of the air with her beak and flew straight to her nest. Subsequent cargo for her construction included more cottonwood seed tufts, pieces of dried grass, discarded bird feathers and more spider webbing. She felted these materials into the nest's walls, binding the work with the webbing. Sometimes she used her little feet to mold the nest. When she changed positions, she lifted from the nest on wing power, rather than shifting on her feet, and then re-settled. Obviously, hummingbird landing gear is minimal, and not up to "taxiing." The same is true of helicopters, which, except for giant military types, have lightweight skids that should be called "perch-ing gear." If a helicopter that is perched on the ground is to move a few yards one way or another, it too takes to the air, flies to the new position, and re-perches.

On the eighth day of nest building the hummingbird hen carried mostly cottonwood tufts. Tuft after tuft went into the nest's bottom and inner walls. That she worked on the nest for so many days may have been in deference to her energy requirements. Where other birds have enough stored energy to make an almost uninterrupted project of nest building, the hummingbird has little reserve and a high-frequency feeding priority that dictates "part-time" nest building.

The second day after completing her nest the hummingbird spent most of her time perched either on the structure's rim or on a nearby branch. I sensed she was near the nest only to be ready for the passage of her first egg. I also noticed that when she hovered at her feeder, her little body was so plump, belly feathers obscured her feet.

One warm afternoon when the hen left her tree to feed, I looked into her nest with a mirror on the end of a painter's telescoping roller handle. From out of nowhere the little hen dropped like a rock to a point about a yard from my feet and acted out a "broken wing" hover across the grass. Her maneuver was finished in seconds and ended when she skittered through the bottom of the cyclone fence. I was so surprised it took a moment for me to realize what had taken place. Re-flection in my mirror showed there were no eggs. Next day, however, one egg was there.

After her first egg arrived, the hummingbird made trips between her nest and a neighbor's house. She hovered up and down the roof's trim. With binoculars I watched her pick small flecks of blue-green paint that was peeling from weathered house trim. The flecks were about the size of a grain of rice. From the house she flew with little paint chips to her nest. There she worked the chips onto the nest's sides, stuccoing just enough of them to break up its outline. The chips closely matched the color of her tree's leaves. Since then it has been my experience that each mother-to-be hummingbird uses whatever

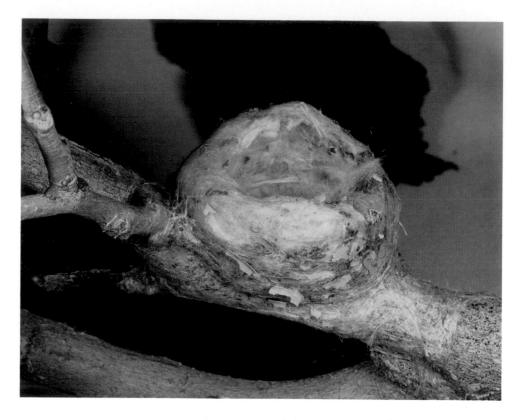

Hummer nest with chips.

local materials best camouflage her nest. Sometimes it is bits of bark, and at other locations it is bits of grass or lichen. Her choice of colors is flawless. An unusual demonstration of how keen the bird is to make her nest melt into its surroundings was a nest built on the dome of a sand-colored Santa Fe style ceramic wind chime. This nest's color, texture, and shape blended so well with the ceramic, the little hen added no camouflage. A twist to this nest camouflage seems to be that the hen doesn't invest in that work until after eggs are laid. Once camouflaging has commenced, it receives continued attention throughout the nest's use (Bowles 1910).

Twenty-four hours after her second egg arrived she began incubating. At this point her body was slim, and her feet were visible again when she hovered at her feeder. During this Black-chinned hummingbird's incubation time I was able to film and watch another Black-chinned nest that was only 5′9″ above the ground.

During incubation, the nest was oblong shaped, matching the form of the hen's body. William Calder has measured hummingbird incubation temperatures at between 95° F and 97° F. The hen, whose body temperature is from 104° F to 109° F, regulates incubation temperature by raising or lowering her body in the nest. When you see a photograph of a brooding hen, if she is low in the nest, forcing her beak and tail feathers to point skyward, the photo was probably taken on a cool day. If the photo shows her high in the nest, it was probably taken on a warm day or when she had chicks.

About every two hours the hen turned her eggs with her beak, often from a hover. When she resettled she rotated her position in the nest that covered an arc between 120 degrees and 180 degrees. During this period, she shaped her nest, almost as though it was made of Spandex. This reshaping was in response to changing temperatures. On cool days, with her beak she molded the top edges inward, to conform to the shape of her body perfectly. On warm days she opened the nest's top, allowing ventilation to maintain optimum incubation temperature. The nest's flexibility reminded me of a drawstring pouch that worked without a string and without bunching. No doubt the nest's ability to stretch or compress was due in large part to her liberal use of spider webbing in its construction.

Two eggs are common for hummingbirds, the same as for eagles. A hummingbird egg is about the size of a pinto bean. Shells are paper thin. I have documented Black-chinned hummingbird egg incubation time to be fourteen days. Other observers have recorded Ruby-throated incubation time to be the same (Prowse 1934; Gessell 1934). Eagle egg incubation time is forty-one. After observing a hummingbird nest I think I understand why Mother Nature apparently decreed that hummingbirds shall lay two eggs.

Growing chicks caused the nest to stretch. The nest's expansion rate matched the chick's growth, thus keeping them consistently snug from the beginning. If there was only one egg, the nest would be less likely to keep a single chick as warm as two. If there were three eggs, three chicks would stretch the nest beyond its limit in four or five days. At that age, three birds would push up, past the warmth of the nest's top edge. That would threaten the chicks, because their body feathers and body biology would not have developed to a point of thermo-regulation. Thermo-regulation is the ability of a chick to maintain its body temperature, independent of its mother's heat. Thermo-regulation, with attendant feather growth, doesn't begin until the chicks are around ten days old. Two growing chicks expand the nest and push up past the top edge at the same time they reach thermo-regulation. It seems Mother Nature and mother hummingbirds made a wise decision about how many eggs should constitute a clutch, and how a nest to serve egg incubation and rapidly growing chicks should be constructed.

Generally the female builds on a small branch about two-thirds the distance from the tree's trunk. Frequently the nest is under the protection of a leaf or a cluster of leaves, often at a fork in the branch. Ruby-throats tend to build on branches overhanging a spring or pond. Increased security may be that bird's motivation for nesting over water. If you have a fish- or duckpond, placing a branch over the pond might encourage Ruby-throats to nest on it.

Once a bird establishes a nest, that site tends to be used year after year. The little hens either rebuild the old nest, build atop an old nest, or build on the same branch if the old nest is gone. We have no proof that it is the same bird nesting in the same site from year to year, but I think it logical to assume so. (From personal experience I know golden eagles reuse their old nests.)

Before I focused on hummingbirds, I had heard their nests are usually around 10 feet above ground. I have since found them as low as eighteen inches above ground (Broad-tails and Calliopes) and as high as thirty-one feet in a cottonwood (Black-chinned). Since hummer nests blend so well into their surroundings, tracking a hen carrying building material is a good method of nest location. Nest building takes the little hen from a few to several days to complete. The Calliope is reputed to be the fastest nest builder. Nesting seasons, variable with latitude, begin mid-April to late May. A nesting schedule for the sixteen species that breed in the U.S. and Canada is listed in the Guide to North American Hummingbirds (p. 89 below).

Nestlings are vulnerable to snakes, praying mantis, roadrunners, wasps, and ants. Against some of these predators I daub a ring of Tanglefoot (The Tanglefoot Co., Grand Rapids, MI) around the main branch supporting a nest's limb, at the tree's trunk. This sticky substance, available at local nurseries, traps ants that may climb a tree. Use with care so that hummingbirds aren't entrapped.

When we consider that a hen carries approximately one thousand loads of sugary nectar into a nest during its season, it is understandable why ants sometimes find their way into her nest.

Some people believe that if a mother hummingbird can't find enough nectar and insects to feed herself and two youngsters, she will abandon her young in favor of her own life. At the other extreme, in a favorable environment she often remates and establishs a second nest, and in the deep southwest, a third. When that occurs, for a few

Ruby-throated female feeding her young.
Photograph by Ed Brown

days the little mother incubates her second clutch between feeding her first, nearly mature chicks. By this time the chicks take turns spending time on the nest's edge to exercise their wings. When they reach this stage of growth, they also occasionally zap a passing gnat, mosquito, or fruit fly that strays near enough the nest to be within range of their lightning-bolt tongues.

When the youngsters practice "flying" within the nest, they hang onto its rim and hum their wings without allowing themselves to become airborne. Practice, and the strength it builds, makes them good flyers when they make their first flight. Often a fledgling must make three or four tries before successfully perching, however, because it hasn't practiced landings.

After her first chicks fly, the hen takes on the double duty of incubating new eggs and feeding newly fledged young. Some of these young birds will return to the area of their birth the next spring. Since hummingbirds live an average of one to three years, you have an opportunity to build your hummingbird population from generational year to generational year.

The longest recorded lifespan of a hummingbird is that of a female Broad-tailed. Twelve years after she was banded by Nickolas Waser, this hummingbird was recaptured at the Rocky Mountain Biological Laboratory, Gothic, Colorado. Ages of other species have been verified by other banders, including a female Ruby-throated in Hollister, Missouri, at nine years and another Ruby-throated in Jay, Oklahoma, at eight. Unfortunately, fossilized hummingbird remains have not been discovered; therefore we don't know exactly how long these tiny birds have been around. An educated guess, however, can be made from fossilized flowers that codeveloped with hummingbirds and are considered to be "hummingbird flowers." These flowers date back about three million years. Eagles have been established, from fossilized remains, as far back as 36 million years.

Hummingbird Predators

The only predator that may specialize in hunting hummingbirds is the tiny hawk, *Accipiter superciliosus fontanieri,* of Costa Rica rain forests (Stiles 1978).

The tiny hawk has been observed capturing Costa Rican hummingbirds by sudden attacks within the hummingbird's territory, rather than sustained aerial pursuit. That tactic seems a reasonable approach to snagging quarry as quick and nimble as a hummer.

In the United States and Canada, as far as is known, there are no specialized hummingbird predators. Predation on hummers seems to occur only when the birds present targets of opportunity, when the nimble hummer is simply in the wrong place at the wrong time. Apparently that happens fairly often.

Orioles, flycatchers, and small hawks and falcons appear to be among the best (or worst, depending on your viewpoint) at snagging hummers. One such account, involving a Baltimore oriole, is given by Bruce Wright, Director, Northwestern Wildlife Station, University of New Brunswick, Fredericton, N.B., Canada.

"My wife and I were watching a male Baltimore oriole on a shrub in our garden on 4 June 1961. Two male orioles had been feeding on blossoms without apparent friction, while two pairs of Ruby-throated hummingbirds also worked over the flowers. A male hummingbird hovered in front of a blossom within about one-third meter of one of the male orioles. The oriole turned, pounced, and caught the hummingbird in its beak. It then flew to a nearby branch and held the hummingbird down with its feet and pecked at it violently until feathers flew from it. When I approached to observe more closely, the oriole flew and dropped the hummingbird to the ground. When I picked the little bird up, it was dead" (Wright 1962).

In August 1976 Philip Ashman of the Point Reyes Bird Observatory in Stinson Beach, California, watched an immature or adult female northern (Bullock's) oriole (*Icterus galbula*) eating a hummingbird. "The oriole held the hummingbird with one foot and tore off and swallowed pieces of muscle from the hummingbird's back. It is not known whether the oriole was a predator or scavenger, since we did not see how it obtained the hummingbird" (Ashman 1977).

In Albuquerque, I have seen Bullock's orioles regularly invade a lilac bush containing one to three perched Black-chinned hummingbirds. In my view, the oriole's bush invasion was aggressive toward the hummingbirds. On the other hand, when this oriole "hovered" at the hummingbird's feeder, occasionally a male Black-chinned zipped down and displayed respectful aggression toward the larger bird.

At Cave Creek Ranch near Portal, Arizona, George Gamboa of the University of Kansas watched a Wied's crested flycatcher kill a male Rufous hummingbird at a feeder. "The flycatcher swooped down from a perch it had used several days near the feeder. The flycatcher extended its wings just prior to midair contact with the hovering hummingbird, and knocked the small bird to the ground. The flycatcher quickly picked up the stunned hummingbird in its beak by one wing and flew to a branch overhanging the feeder. The Rufous dangled from the flycatcher's beak. Repeatedly, the flycatcher knocked the hummingbird against the branch with violent side to side motions of its head. The flycatcher then flew with its prey out of my vision to a distant tree" (Gamboa 1977).

Also in Arizona, Carroll Peabody, along with a visiting class of schoolchildren and their teacher, saw a brown-crested flycatcher descend on a hummingbird feeding at the Mile Hi (Ramsey Canyon). Peabody said the flycatcher snapped the hovering bird out of the air in front of a feeder with its beak, in regular flycatcher fashion, and flew away with its catch. Larger birds of prey also take hummingbirds.

An eastern pigeon hawk (*Falco columbarius columbarius*) collected by George Lowery, Jr., at Grand Isle, Louisiana, in 1937 was found to have in its stomach "the identifiable remains of a Ruby-throated hummingbird" (Lowery 1938).

In 1963, Hans Peeters of the Museum of Vertebrate Zoology,

Berkeley, California, noted, ". . . the display flight of a male Anna's hummingbird above a dense growth of *seep* one-half mile east of Berkeley. After the flight the bird perched on a dead branch protruding above one of the bushes and preened. At the same time a male sharp-shinned hawk (*Accipiter striatus*) flew rapidly along the *Baccharis* toward the hummingbird. The hawk dashed along about one foot above the ground, apparently using the brush as a screen. When it was approximately opposite the hummingbird, it suddenly swooped up over the bushes and seized the Anna's. In doing so the hawk barely checked its flight, and flew on to a stand of Baytrees (*Umbelluraia californica*), where it disappeared" (Peeters 1963).

Sparrow hawks (American kestrel, *Falco sparverius*) also prey on hummingbirds. This account comes from Ernst Mayr of the Museum of Comparative Zoology, Harvard University, Cambridge, Massachusetts. ". . . together with Mrs. Mayr and two friends, I was watching through a window a Ruby-throated hummingbird feeding on zinnias at Lyndeboro, New Hampshire. Suddenly a sparrow hawk plunged down to the flower bed about a foot away from the hummingbird and with a flash-like sideward movement caught the hummingbird with its feet. The hawk immediately rose steeply and was already about 100 feet high when, within a few seconds, I had reached the outside. The ability of these birds to strike prey on the wing is perhaps greater than known" (Mayr 1966).

Bob Cooper told me of seeing an immature Cooper's hawk pursue a Broad-tailed hummingbird one afternoon in the Sandia mountains near Albuquerque, at Los Huertas, during a time with threatening clouds. The little bird was nimble enough to escape; the hawk missed a turn and lost feathers in a scrape with a fence. Bob added that at about that same time hail began falling, and it wasn't until half an hour after the hail stopped that the hummingbirds reemerged.

So many observations of aerial attacks against hummingbirds by larger birds suggest these attacks are not infrequent. This could be why most hummingbirds, especially females, have a lot of green on their backs. Such coloration would blend the bird with vegetation below, rendering them more difficult to be seen by predators from above. Although green coloring may help against attackers from above, in pond areas amphibians strike from below.

An account of a frog killing a female Rufous hummingbird is related by Morgan Monroe. The location was upper Cave Creek Canyon about two miles west of the American Museum of Natural History's Southwestern Research Station in Arizona's Chiricahua Mountains.

Morgan states, "My wife and I were at a small lake impounded by Herb Martyr Dam in Cochise County, Arizona. As we sat on the north bank of the lake observing birds, the hummingbird, [probably] a migrant, perched on a partly submerged tree branch, then flew down and landed at the edge of the water about 30 feet in front of us. Apparently the bird sought a drink; it dipped its mandibles into the shallow water once after landing. Immediately a frog of unidentified species leaped from the grass near the water line, struck the bird a hard blow and knocked it into deeper water. The bird struggled in several inches of water as the frog followed up its initial attack by seizing the bird and diving with it into a bed of submerged vegetation. Neither bird nor frog reappeared on the surface. We searched for some 15 minutes without success in an effort to locate them. Whether frogs regularly take hummingbirds under like circumstances or whether the bird was mistaken for a large insect is unknown" (Monroe 1957).

In Canada, leopard frogs apparently help themselves to hummingbirds. L.S.T. Norris gives these three accounts:

(1) "At Gull Harbor, about ninety miles from the south end of Lake Winnipeg, a man said he and a companion saw a large frog leap at and capture a hummingbird they were watching. The bird was hovering at a flower when seized."

(2) "Near Portage la Prairie, a man observed a large frog take a hummingbird while the bird hovered at a flower."

(3) "Hugh Moncrieff, a Winnipeg naturalist and nature photographer, was watching a male Ruby-throated hummingbird among flowers at his cottage in Gimli in 1939. While appraising the situation for photography, Moncrieff heard a snap and saw a frog fall on the flower border while at the same time the bird had disappeared. With the help of boys the frog was captured and killed. As the boys dissected the amphibian, Moncrieff filmed the hummingbird body's recovery" (Norris 1944).

Frog attacks against hummingbirds may be more common than previously suspected. For example, at the Jimmy Swartz place on the Nueces River near Corpus Christi, Texas, I filmed migrating Ruby-throated hummingbirds on September 20, 1992. Two feeders for luring birds to my camera were set 36 inches above the ground. As I filmed, it became common for as many as three Rio-Grande leopard frogs (Rana berlandieri) to hop from the cover of turk's cap and gather below hummingbirds swarming around my camera's feeders. Leaping as high as 34 inches, the frogs attempted to grab hummers out of the air.

Several of the hummingbirds I filmed were mising all or part of their tail feathers. During the day, the birds fed at turk's cap blossoms around the Swartz home. In and around these plants, leopard frogs lurked, and Jimmy's son Glenn said he found three or four frogs trying to swallow a hummingbird. I think an intelligent assumption is, the tail-less hummingbirds lost their feathers to near misses by leaping Rio-Grande leopard frogs. Since leopard frogs are common in the United States, Canada, and much of Mexico (California, Oregon, Washington, and British Columbia are exceptions), it seems fair to speculate that leopard frogs take a significant number of foraging hummingbirds.

Other attacks on hummingbirds have been more bizarre.

In July 1939, James Grant of Vernon, British Columbia, was watching a Rufous hummingbird fly among flowers in a garden at Trinity Valley, B.C. (Grant 1955). Grant reports, "The bird suddenly uttered a sharp squeak and dropped into the foliage. Approaching where the bird disappeared, I found it lying belly down on the ground with its eyes closed and wings half spread. As I bent to pick it up the head of a black hornet, *Vespula maculata* (L.), with its mandibles working furiously, appeared between the bird's rectrices. The insect fled at almost the same moment it came into view. Then the hummingbird took wing and disappeared over the treetops in an almost vertical flight.

"I have often wondered if the hornet actually stung the bird, in which case the result would surely have been fatal; or if the insect's onslaught had caused the bird to become paralyzed with fright. As we knew of no hornet's nest in the vicinity, the attack apparently was an act of aggression rather than one of defense."

Grant continues, "An instance of yellow jackets, *Vespula* probably *arenaria* (Fab), preying upon hummingbirds was observed in the same locality. We had found the nest of a Rufous hummingbird. One day soon after the young birds hatched we were dismayed to find them being consumed by wasps. It was a summer memorable for its plague of wasps and perhaps not surprising that this nest failed to escape the hordes of persistent foragers."

As if orioles, flycatchers, hawks, frogs, and wasps weren't enough, praying mantis also prey on hummingbirds. Here are two examples.

Earl Hildebrand, of Texas A & M University, says, "In September 1948, my neighbor, Mrs. O.K. Smith, heard a shrill bird-call early one evening. Upon checking, she saw several Ruby-throated hummingbirds circling a blossom. The cry came from one bird that was gripped by a praying mantis poised on a flower. Mrs. Smith grasped the struggling bird, whereupon it collapsed in her hands. Mrs. Smith said there was a spot of blood on its head; however, the bird soon revived and flew" (Hildebrand 1949).

A second observer of a hummingbird-praying mantis encounter reports a negative outcome for the hummer.

In Philadelphia, Pennsylvania, Christella Butler saw a mantis poised on an orange-colored zinnia one late afternoon in September 1948. Butler reports, "When a hummingbird flew to the flower, the mantis seized the bird. I hastened to rescue the hummingbird, but even after both had been removed to the ground the mantis would not release its hold. As I forcibly separated the two, bits of feathers held by the mantis were torn from the bird. The hummingbird was dead. The only blood was from its bill" (Butler 1949).

In the southwest, roadrunners also grab hummingbirds. This account comes from Sally Hoyt Spofford, of Portal, Arizona. "On April 28, 1974, my husband and I were photographing hummingbirds at our window feeders. We became aware that one of our resident pair of roadrunners was crouched on the roof of a small porch nine feet above ground, just above some hummingbird feeders. We had seen the roadrunner on the ground below the feeders, occasionally leaping into the air in an unsuccessful attempt to catch a hummingbird. Crouched on the porch roof, the roadrunner changed position several times when hummingbirds were at the feeder. Once in a while the desert bird made tentative passes at a hummingbird. Suddenly it leaped from the roof and snapped up a hovering Black-chin, landing on the ground with the hummingbird in its beak."

Mrs. Spofford continues, "Then, on June 20, 1974, we saw a roadrunner pounding something on the ground under where we had several oriole and hummingbird feeders hanging from low branches. We approached the roadrunner, which ran a short distance and dropped its prey. Its prey was a Black-chinned hummingbird that died in less than a minute" (Spofford 1976).

In Red Rock, New Mexico, Alton Ford reports a roadrunner that snapped up two hummingbirds while crouched on a window sill next to a feeder in 1990. Ford is a New Mexico state game farm manager.

At my home in Albuquerque, circumstantial evidence suggests a roadrunner ate two eggs from a Black-chinned hummingbird's nest. While the Black-chin's first nest was under construction, a roadrunner flew into the hummingbird's tree and walked the limb on which the female was building a nest. After the roadrunner's walk, the hummingbird abandoned work at that site and began a new nest in a neighboring tree.

The height above ground of the Black-chin's second nest was triple that of the first. However, soon after her eggs were laid, they were violated by an unknown attacker. Under that circumstance, it may be premature to implicate the roadrunner, since a snake (or oriole, or something else) could have eaten the eggs. Snakes are a problem for nesting birds. Peabody in Tucson told of an incident where he found a snake moving along a limb toward a hummingbird nest. That hummingbirds may recognize their danger from snakes is shown by a snake-hummingbird incident seen by J.H. Bowles in the Santa Barbara, California, area.

"I noticed a female Anna's making repeated dives into the center of a wild rose bush. I looked for what had her attention and found a four-foot coral snake. With the hummingbird watching from a neighboring live oak perch, I killed the snake. Its stomach contents showed it was guilty of nothing more than eating a lizard.

"I tossed the snake on the ground near the bush and moved a short distance away to see what the hummer would do. Almost immediately the Anna's darted down and hovered over the reptile. Cautiously she gradually dropped lower, until she was no more than a foot above the snake. Her head was bent down. Her caution, in contrast to female Anna hummingbird behavior, showed she may have appreciated her danger. Hovering from point to point, the hummingbird examined the snake from several angles before whirling up into the air, and away.

"Her behavior toward the dead snake was so different from when it was alive I believed the hummingbird was satisfied the snake was dead, therefore discounting it as a problem" (Bowles 1910).

Spiderwebs could hardly be classed as predators; nevertheless, hummingbirds sometimes become entangled in them with predatory results. Robert Woods reported a 1934 entangling incident in Azusa, California. "I encountered a female or immature Costa hanging head downward, with folded wings, by two strands of a nearly demolished web of our largest common orb weaver spider. The bird looked dead, but when taken in hand it opened its beak and struggled feebly. I under-took removal of the web, which was well wrapped around its wings. The strands were so tough and viscid that unentangling was difficult and risked pulling out feathers.

"Released, the bird was too exhausted to fly, so I took it inside a room. A few minutes later it was found clinging to a window screen.

When taken to a doorway, the hummingbird flew, apparently in good health" (Woods 1934).

Woods points out that orb spiders spin a particularly coarse thread that often spans ten feet or more. He concludes that a hummingbird in full flight would break through the orb's webbing without harm. "But if it should blunder in while hovering, the beating of its wings might easily wrap about it a large portion of the web; and such is the strength of the fabric that it seems capable of holding a bird of considerably larger size."

An Anna's caught in a spiderweb was observed by Ken Stott, Jr., of the Zoological Society of San Diego, California. Stott writes, "June 7, 1950, Charles Shaw of the San Diego Zoo's department of reptiles summoned staff members to witness a remarkable spectacle in a landscaped area behind the reptile house. An immature male Anna hummingbird had become entangled in the web of an orb-weaver spider.

"The bird was suspended by the left wing from a point near the center of a horizontal span of web measuring approximately nine feet from end to end and at a height of approximately seven and a half feet from the ground. In an attempt to free itself, the bird, using its free right wing, flew in a swinging circular manner and in so doing further bound the primaries of the enmeshed wing in the web. During its struggle, it called frequently, attracting another Anna hummingbird which hovered in the vegetation nearby. In one instance the flying hummer, which appeared to be female, approached to within two feet of the trapped bird.

"For more than forty minutes the bird attempted unsuccessfully to free itself. With each successive effort, it became more firmly entangled and showed increasing signs of exhaustion. It seemed most unlikely the bird would be able to free itself; consequently, Shaw cut the web, unwound the portion that had wrapped around the bird's primaries, and released the hummer" (Stott 1951).

Lizards are another hazard to hummingbirds. In Gila, New Mexico, Steve McDonald told of an incident that occurred in May 1989. In Steve's words, "I had placed a dead piñon pine in our flower garden. The tree had character and I considered it decorative. From one of the piñon's dead limbs I suspended a hummingbird feeder. After I saw hummingbird feathers under the tree I began to watch activity around the feeder.

"One May afternoon a Clark's spiny lizard grabbed a Black-chin hummingbird in its jaws when the bird came near the feeder. The lizard was on the bottom of the limb, and blended so well it was nearly impossible to see. Once I saw what was happening, I realized the feeder was too near the limb. Relocating the feeder to a position where feeding hummers would be out of reach of lizards solved the problem."

In the Mimbres mountains 30 miles north of Silver City, New Mexico, Dave Seymour saw an unidentified 5- to 6-inch lizard carrying a Black-chinned hummingbird. Dave doesn't know if the reptile scavenged or killed that hummer.

In Rockport, Texas, I talked with shrimp boat captains who described seeing seagulls force hummingbirds to the water, then circle and grab the struggling hummer with their beaks. Other boat crewmen said they had seen seagulls fly up behind low-flying hummers and snap them out of the air with their beaks. It seems logical to assume seagulls snag hummingbirds on our east and west coasts as well.

We don't normally consider mid-air collisions a hazard for hummingbirds. However, Bill Calder describes such an incident.

Calder noticed a Broad-tailed with a bee skewered on its beak. Apparently the bird was cruising at high speed when it and the bee met on a collision course. The bee's body clamped the hummer's beak shut. Bill and his teams have banded more hummingbirds than anyone in the world (7,000 plus as of summer 1991.) Their expertise enabled them to use hummingbird trapping equipment, catch the bird, remove the bee, and set an undoubtedly happy hummer free. In Montana there was another case of a hummingbird that pierced an insect with its beak.

In Swan Lake, Montana, hummingbird bander Elly Jones captured a female Rufous that had skewered a black-colored wasp on its beak, August 10, 1991. In Elly's words, "The insect had dried like cement around her beak." Most Rufous Elly weighed tipped her scales an average of 4.09 g. The wasp-hampered Rufous weighed only three quarters of that. Elly chipped the wasp's carcass away with small scissors and fed the bird. After placing band #T51753 on its leg, she released the Rufous and it zoomed off into the world. Considering the Rufous' personality, it's possible the little bird lanced the wasp deliberately.

Hummingbirds share a relationship with a mite that is interesting. This mite feeds and reproduces in flowers. However, the mites depend upon hummingbirds to transport them from one flower to another. The mites do this by quickly running onto the beak of a hummingbird while it feeds. Once aboard, the critters hurry into the bird's nostrils. Later, while the hummingbird feeds at another flower, the mites scurry from the hummingbird's nostrils, down its beak, and onto the new flower. Rarely does a hummingbird carry more than a dozen of these quick little hitchhikers (Colwell & Naeem 1979). (Is this hummingbird/mite connection a hint at interdependencies we know nothing of that may exist between other living creatures?)

A danger to hummingbirds in the form of electric fencing was suggested to me. Because the birds examine things red, it was rumored that they were sometimes electrocuted while inspecting red electric fence insulators. My physics background raised suspicion about this idea. To confirm or refute the electric fence and hummingbird electrocution proposition I bought a fence charger.

After experimenting with the device, and exposing hummingbirds to it, it is my opinion that electric fencing poses no unusual threat to hummingbirds. The fence is charged with only 12 volts DC and 1.5 amps. Neither of these amounts is likely to be lethal to a hummingbird. But more importantly, these fences are designed to shock an animal that is simultaneously standing on the ground and touching the charged (hot) fence wire, thereby completing an electrical circuit. If a fence is properly installed, no hummingbird could grasp the wire and stand on the ground at the same time. Therefore, the bird couldn't complete a circuit. (Wet insulators, wires, and posts might be a different story.)

Emotionally, it sounds as if an electric fence would be dangerous to hummingbirds. In reality I find, mercifully, it isn't. Nor for that matter is a properly installed electric fence dangerous to meadowlarks, doves, lark buntings, and hundreds of other birds that perch on such fences.

A potential hazard to migrating hummingbirds is plastic flowers placed on graves. Picture for a moment a nearly exhausted young hummer searching for nectar. Imagine the bird happening upon a large cemetery. Then imagine a tired bird proceeding from plastic flower to plastic flower, growing more tired with each visit, until at the base of a plastic flower replica the little bird drops, too exhausted to fly anymore.

Loss of habitat is a threat to hummers. In South Texas, especially between Corpus Christi and Brownsville, so much natural habitat has been lost to agriculture there is less and less nectar for hummingbirds. This area is a major migration route for untold numbers of Ruby-throats (and others) each spring and fall. From Brownsville to Corpus Christi, feeders would reduce migration stresses on these birds.

All About Hummers

Hummingbirds and Water

In Palo Duro Canyon, the small spring near my eagle blind poured over rocks that created small "waterfalls." At those falls the humming-birds gathered to bathe. Watching these petite birds splash and bathe on a rock under trickling water was amusing and charming. It was obvious the little birds liked water, and since none made territorial claims, apparently the water was community property. Back home in Albuquerque, I told a group of friends, including Native Americans, about the ritual. Indian friends chuckled knowingly, and told of their *kachina* dolls fashioned with hummingbird-shaped heads. The dolls' heads had long slender beaks and multicolored feathers. For years I had seen these *kachinas* in southwestern gift shops without knowing the symbolism behind their design. Thanks to hummers, I now know these hummingbird *kachinas* are a spiritual tribute to a bird many Indians regard as their "rain bird." Because hummingbirds are the only bird I know that regularly flies in rain, the Indian association with hummingbirds and rain makes perfect sense. Other Native Americans called hummingbirds "the sunbeam bird," probably because of how gorgets respond to sunlight.

A plausible reason for hummingbirds flying in rain may be tied to their energy requirements. Where other birds can wait out rain for hours, even days in the case of eagles, before hunger drives them to feed, hummingbird metabolism rates are so high the birds must feed often, rain or shine.

On cold, rainy days, a male Black-chinned I regularly watch hunkers under a dry, snug branch in a cedar next to the porch between feedings. I take the hummingbird's action to mean he has sense enough to get out of a cold rain and flies in it only because he is hungry. This same bird will perch directly in a warm rain, and seems to enjoy it. However, another male reduces his rain flying time by cruising under the protection of a carport and adjoining covered porch on rainy-day trips to and from a feeder. This hummingbird's action seems to say it would rather fly dry, if given a choice. I have also seen several hummingbird nests under a sheltering porch, shed roof, or inside barns.

All this hummingbirds-and-water history inspired me to install a hose that dribbled water onto a flat rock in a sunny corner of my yard. During spring the birds paid little attention to the water, but when summer came, it was a hit. Later, Joanne Phillips of Albuquerque told of a Black-chinned that poised in the air next to the stream of water

Kachina Doll.

from a hose she was using to water grass. The bird studied the flow a moment, then "landed on the stream and rode it almost to the ground before zipping back to repeat his ride." And Joan Day Martin, of Albuquerque, watched Broad-tailed hummingbirds drop to her birdbath's water and skim along like skittering ducks.

Before California's severe water shortage, my sister in Mission Viejo told of a refinement for a normal birdbath that Anna's seem to like: water barely flowing over a birdbath's lip suits the little fellows. They sat on the lip and dipped into shallow overflow. My sister reports that when the birds gyrated their wet wings, the spray often produced miniature rainbows. In light of water shortages, a circulating system that is miserly in its water use may be acceptable. A second

49

hummingbird bath can be created that uses no additional water by placing a flat stone under the overflow, within the system's circulation loop. Generally, hummingbirds seem to prefer the splash or mist from dripping or falling water to a geyser or fountain of water.

I have heard of hummers bathing in a leaf wet with rainwater or dew. Since leaves that large are rare in the southwest, I substituted a small seashell partially filled with water. A few of the little birds seemed to appreciate the seashell tub, but their main preference continued to be running or splashing water. At the Jimmy Swartz home near Corpus Christi, Texas, I saw what I consider the ultimate hummingbird water system.

Jimmy's son, Glenn, punched a small needle hole in a plastic cap fitted to the male end of a garden hose. The small water stream was directed into the middle of a leafy bush six to eight feet away. Mini waterfalls fell from leaf ends, creating waters that hummingbirds frolicked in as I've seen nowhere else. (Heat the needle before pushing into the plastic cap. Make a very small hole; it not only conserves water, but it takes very little water from this system to make hummers happy.)

During extreme heat in the desert southwest, a fog mister continually misting air around a feeder creates a micro-airconditioned environment hummingbirds flock to. Perches in these evaporative cooled spaces are popular with the birds on days when temperatures soar above 100° F. A mister serves the birds by refreshing them and simultaneously providing a mini-bath. Fogger-misters are available through garden supply houses or nurseries. Use, of course, depends on an area's water availability, since this system is nonrecirculating.

Sticky nectar and pollen are probably one reason behind the hummingbird's affinity for water. When the birds lap nectar from flowers it seems reasonable to assume that as they probe a flower's depths, surplus syrup and pollen may coat their bills, the sides of their heads and throats, and maybe even their wing roots. Water solves their hygiene problem. Water for hummingbirds to bathe in is essential for keeping feathers in top condition, which contributes to the bird's survival. In that regard, most feeders are cleaner for hummingbirds to feed from than flowers. This is especially true if a feeder's bee guards and artificial corollas have been removed. A further advantage to providing water is that such an environment encourages the birds not only to reside, but to nest nearby.

Feeding
Hummingbirds

Feeder Timing

If you have never hung a hummingbird feeder, consider this: it is probable that sometime during the season nearly every square yard of the continental United States, and much of Canada, is inspected by a hummingbird. More importantly, a feeder offers hummingbirds the daily equivalent of nectar found in the 2,000–5,000 flowers each bird must otherwise visit every day. A properly prepared feeder is a hummingbird bonanza.

It is important to have feeders up a few days before birds are expected. Feeders should be in place early so as not to miss the first-to-arrive males. My experience with Black-chinned hummingbirds is that males show up shopping for a territory. One or more will stop where they find a feeder. The bonus comes a few days later when females and last year's young join the males and feed.

If you attract more than one male and would like to "keep" them all, immediately hang a feeder for each male. These additional feeders should be out of sight and/or some distance from each other. Squabbles will settle which male claims which nectar gold mine as his territory. Females will be drawn to a male on a territory. Between feedings the birds may fly off to perch in your neighbor's yard, either across the street or down the block. You increase the chance of them staying nearby if you provide perches near your feeders.

After other feeders are in place, the birds will continue squabbling, but on a level that says there is enough for all. Generally, the more feeders you place, the more birds you will attract. The following story of a missed opportunity came to me in Pampa, Texas.

Carolyn Kessel, who was considering setting out a feeder for the first time, related how in early spring she saw a hummingbird flying around her flower garden, which was not yet in bloom. The hummer hummed from bush to bush, hovering at spots where blossoms had been last fall. When it found no flowers, and no feeder, the bird left.

For the rest of that spring Carolyn saw no other hummingbirds. Had she had a feeder up, it is probable the scout would have stayed, along with following females. The early feeder gets the hummingbird.

Carolyn vowed that next year her feeder will be up a week before birds are likely to arrive.

In July, Carolyn put up her feeders. In late July and early August, southbound migrants paused at her place and helped themselves to sugar water. Chances are excellent that some of these birds will check her place next spring, and stay with her through the summer if they find sugar water waiting.

After you have attracted birds, if you must be absent longer than their liquid will last or remain fresh, it is important that you appoint someone to keep your feeders serviced. An example of how hummingbirds react to properly serviced feeders comes from Steve and Anne Trigg, on their 60,000 acre ranch in the break country of eastern New Mexico.

In 1973, when Anne moved to the ranch, there were four Black-chinned hummingbirds coming to a single feeder. By 1991, her hummingbird population was estimated at 300. Anne attributes their success at attracting hummingbirds to diligent feeding, and keeping several one-quart feeders clean. Since the Trigg ranch has no standout geographical guiding line, such as a major river, or a range of mountains, the increase in hummingbirds may be a generational pyramid. If so, the Trigg ranch could be a destination point each spring for a unique group of Black-chins that winter somewhere in Mexico. This flock of possibly related hummingbirds, along with Rufous migrants in the fall, might make a revealing study about hummingbird migration. Feeders at the ranch are kept up in the fall until the last bird is gone.

In some circles it is suggested that feeders be taken down in the fall because it is believed that the birds would become dependent and "forget" to migrate. Disagreement persists on that hypothesis. Some experts believe that feeders available to hummingbirds at migrating time have little or no influence on their leaving. These experts contend that decreasing daylight triggers biochemical messages to the birds' brains overriding the attraction of a food supply. Other experts believe that declining insect populations are the primary cause for birds to move south, regardless of nectar availability.

In Albuquerque, I leave feeders up in the fall until there are no birds left, which generally happens early in October in the valley. So far I haven't observed a healthy hummer that forgot to migrate. Lee Gass of Vancouver answers, "But you are in the south," and points out that he knows of instances in Canada where Rufous hummingbirds were stranded in the fall. He says, "They were hooked on feeders.

For example, people in British Columbia strand hummers because the flowers and insects dry up farther south while the feeders still do fine." Gass believes leaving feeders up too late into fall is a problem in all northern areas.

A conclusive study is needed. Until someone does that we are left to use our own best judgments about when to take feeders down in the fall. Notice I used the term "healthy hummer" when I said I hadn't seen a hummingbird that failed to migrate in the fall. There is more to the story.

One December day I received a call from Donnie and Harrett Watkins in Amarillo, Texas, about a sub-adult male Anna's that had stayed at a feeder. (Although Anna's have been reported in warmer parts of Texas, this is the first recorded in the Panhandle.) The Watkinses said the bird's tongue had been sticking out of its beak into the winter air for "a long time." I drove for Amarillo through light snow.

From the Watkinses' warm kitchen we watched the bird come to a window feeder. Sure enough, a lot of the Anna's tongue flapped in the winter breeze. Half of the bird's beak was broken off.

It took the bird a long time to gather sugar water through its broken beak. Barely able to hover in its weakened condition, it was a pathetic hummer that seemed to be just hanging on. After feeding, he perched on a vine under an eave, probably the warmest place he could find.

Donnie said the bird's beak had not grown since they first noticed its condition. Reduced beak growth probably resulted from a lack of protein, because there were no insects for the bird in Amarillo's December. We formed a plan for the Anna's recovery.

First we installed a perch on the feeder so the little guy could sit while he fed. Lack of insect nutrients was made up by adding liquid protein (10-grain gelatin capsules) to a higher than normal ratio of sugar to water. (Since then I have learned of a very good but very expensive commercial hummingbird mix for sick hummers from Germany used by the San Diego zoo called Nec-ton). We kept the solution warm in their feeder with a heat lamp. Almost immediately the little bird looked less bedraggled.

Within a week the broken beak was growing rapidly and a lot less tongue flowed in the cold air. Where he was perching for the night was a mystery. Our next move, on a day that turned snowy and 20° with winds blowing thirty, was to coax the bird into the Watkinses' horse barn with a heated feeder. The inside feeder, plus heat from the horses and a heat lamp, kept the hummingbird snug on cold days.

It appeared the damaged hummer was going to make it through the winter. I even envisioned the little bird migrating on schedule next fall. Unfortunately, one night the hummingbird's droppings fell onto his heat lamp. The lamp exploded, panicking the bird (and horses) out into a 7° night. We didn't see the hummer again.

Looking back, I believe if the Watkinses had taken their feeder down early, it would have been difficult for the disabled bird to have survived migration. It is possible that the broken-beak hummingbird lived into the Panhandle December because it stayed with the security of a feeder. (Does this imply that at least some hummingbirds are capable of "sensible" decisions that override instinct?) It is my opinion that if you have a fall straggler, it could be straggling because it may not feel up to par; it may not have stored enough fat reserves; or it could be a second or third brood (late hatched) youngster still growing, and not ready for the demands of a migratory flight. In my view, taking a feeder down would deny these hummingbirds the option of waiting to migrate until they felt fit for the trip. There may be a flip side to that coin, however.

Suppose the stragglers are birds that natural selection is attempting to weed from the hummingbird gene pool. Suppose a majority of the stragglers are in some way imperfect, whose genes Mother Nature intends to freeze out of existence, to the species' benefit. Is it possible that by leaving feeders up, we dilute the hummingbird gene pool with less than perfect specimens, against Mother Nature's design? Suppose the brain chemistry of some of these stragglers has been altered by environmental hazards we created. Is it possible some of these stragglers are an omen, in the way that eagle population changes (and hawks and owls) along Hawk Mountain were the DDT omen? Each fall I wrestle with these thoughts. On balance, I think leaving feeders up gives hummingbirds sugar water beacons as they belatedly, for whatever reason, move south. New information could change my mind about bringing in feeders in the fall, but for now, I plan to leave them up until I'm reasonably sure all stragglers have safely passed. There is one exception that hummingbird expert Bill Baltosser, formerly of the University of New Mexico and now at the University of Arkansas, believes is important.

In the extreme southern portions of our southern states—Arizona, New Mexico, Texas, Louisiana, Mississippi, Alabama, Georgia and Florida—it is Bill's conviction that feeders should be taken down in the fall. His reasoning is that it is possible to "hook" migrating hummingbirds on feeders during an unusually warm fall. Warm, summer-like weather, plus feeder food, may convince the little birds they have gone far enough south . . . that they are safe from the threat of winter. Then when a twenty- or thirty-year record cold blast hits, say in the middle of the night, a significant number of those birds may be lost in one swoop. Bill's opinion is not based on a study, since there are none. It is simply his gut feeling, plus the statement he hears from local people after a frigid blast in those far southern zones: "Overnight, the birds just disappeared."

Obviously, the hummingbirds either flew south on frantic wings or they died during a sudden onslaught of the elements. With the question open, it might be wise to deactivate feeders by mid-October in that narrow southern zone of the southern states. In Canada and extreme northern states it might be wise to consider feeder deactivation when it is time for hummingbirds to migrate south.

Feeder Placement

Hummers that came to a feeder I once hung under an eave of my house seemed edgy. Invariably they approached the feeder via staging points. From their last staging point they dashed to the feeder, fed hurriedly, and dashed away. After watching these comings and goings I concluded the little guys felt crowded by the eave's overhang. I suspected a lot of uneasiness they showed when feeding under an overhang came from not being able to spot, as early as possible, the approach of a rival bird in attack mode. Additionally, the closed upper airspace caused by the eave might have made them nervous about not being able to zip straight up if need be . . . possibly to escape the paws of a house cat. Since hummingbirds fly backwards,* sideways, *and* straight up, it made sense that they might feel more comfortable where they could see more and be able to employ all of their flight skills. To test this theory, a couple of yards farther down the eave I nailed a 1″ × 2″ board to its underside.

---

*The Scottish Duke of Argyle (George Douglas Campbell, 1823–1900) was certain hummingbirds could not fly backwards. He believed hummingbirds *fell* backwards, away from flowers, because it was "impossible for a bird to fly backward." So in 1866 the Duke decreed in his *Reign of Law*, page 145, in italics: "*No bird can ever fly backward.*" In other words, the Duke made it illegal for hummingbirds to fly backward within the Duke's domain. His decree may have been a power play meant to silence (scotch?) points of view differing from his.

Does the Duke's law mean that any hummingbird daring to fly backward is a little rebel?

The board extended a couple of feet out into open air. Making certain there remained ample airspace for sideways and backward flight I suspended a second feeder from the board's outer end. That done, I sat back and watched to see if the birds preferred one feeder over the other.

The extended feeder attracted more birds than the unit under the eave and the birds skipped previous staging points and approached the extended feeder more directly. While feeding, they seemed more relaxed. (For suspending feeders under tree limbs, follow the same guidelines regarding airspace. Keep in mind that tree-mounted feeders are more likely to attract ants.) Satisfied with the hummer's reactions I extended the first feeder. After both feeders were on extensions I had more birds than ever.

As mentioned earlier, when hummingbirds frequent a feeder, invariably one bird tends to drive others away. To understand the so-called feistiness of hummingbirds, keep in mind that these birds have the highest energy demands of all warm-blooded creatures. If we had to eat 100 percent of our weight daily to stay alive, we too would probably be feisty toward interlopers on our food source.

To meet energy demands, the little birds must feed from every five minutes to an hour, depending on air temperature and an individual bird's activity. Having to feed so often probably explains why they fly in ordinary rain that grounds other birds. But rain or shine, the bird's feisty actions around a feeder tended to reduce their numbers in my yard. A solution to that problem was simple.

When I had only one feeder, an aggressive bird had little trouble keeping my hummingbird population low. After I installed a second feeder, the dominant bird continued to terrorize other hummers that approached his domain. In an attempt to solve that problem I widened the distance between feeders. That kept him busier; however, he continued to harass other hummingbirds. Then I introduced a third feeder, far enough from the others to magnify his defense problem. That move was a winner.

Physically, the harassing bird had difficulty protecting three feeders. He was forced to more or less pick one. Even so, what was probably an alpha bird continued to try and harass others at all feeders, with a degree of success. My strategy against that was to hang different kinds of feeders . . . no two alike, and none closer to another than fifteen feet. That move was effective in increasing my hummer population. Once in a while, the dominant bird again patrolled his old territories and harassed targets of opportunity. An even better move was to place more feeders, each out of sight from the others.

Feeder Placement

After I had a number of different kinds of feeders a proper distance apart, the numbers and varieties of hummingbirds attracted to my yard increased. Four feeders are better than three, and so on. And if you live in a multi-species zone, placing one feeder well away from others will often attract the rare bird that might otherwise pass up congested feeders. In that same vein, if you plant flowers for hummingbirds, create three or more major areas of flowers, each far enough apart to diminish an alpha male's ability to dominate more than one flower territory.

These birds seem imprinted into remembering feeder locations from one year to the next, so feeders are best placed in exactly the same location. In spring, since most birds arrive from the south, newcomers will easily find feeders that are on the south side of a building. During fall, feeders on the north side of buildings will have their highest visibility to southward-migrating birds.

The best place for a feeder, from the hummingbird's viewpoint, is an outside corner of a house, for many of the same reasons service stations and fast food outlets are commonly located on corners. Extend the feeder out a couple of feet past the eave. On square homes, obviously three-fourths of the feeders are visible from any one corner. Of the five feeders around my home, invariably the outside corner feeders are empty first. Coincidentally, these extended corner locations provide the best visibility for hummingbirds to spot rivals.

A note about birds that show up "early" in late winter, at the precise place where a feeder hung the previous year: observers have noticed that an extended warm spell in late winter sometimes brings the birds in unexpectedly early. For example, on the 28th of February a lady in Springfield, Missouri, who for years put up feeders in April, had a hummingbird hover at the window where she hangs a feeder each year. (It is possible, especially for a bird returning a second or third year, that its memory of a plentiful food source overrides its sense of season.) Hanging a feeder in late winter for these early arrivals (Sooners?) may become a problem if the weather changes to winter cold and the bird has become dependent. In case of an extremely early arrival you can closely watch five-day weather forecasts and use your judgment about feeding or not feeding. Hummingbird biologists believe that, left unfed, dangerously early arrivals probably have sense enough to turn tail on a cold blast and gyrate their little wings back to warmer areas.

Placing a feeder in front of a window may not be a hummingbird's first choice of location, but they will come there. A window placement can certainly add to your enjoyment of hummingbird watching.

Often, when a bird sees its reflection (or shadow), it will buzz the reflection or shadow with tail feathers spread and wings humming.

Although hummers occasionally fly into patio glass doors, I've seen no problem with these maneuverable little birds colliding with average-sized windows. The key to collision avoidance seems related to window size. The smaller the window, the smaller the problem, and vice versa. However, if you find a collision victim, please retrieve and freeze its body, ants and all if there are any, then contact a hummingbird expert. The bird's remains will provide positive identification on the species. That in turn may significantly add to the store of hummingbird knowledge. Many previously unknown hummingbirds have been so identified. Also check the victim's leg to see if it has been banded.

Wind is a consideration in feeder placement. A sheltered location is desirable, but only so long as sheltering structures don't restrict the birds' airspace and visibility preferences. In mountain pass areas, where localized canyon winds can be fierce and last hours, removing feeders to a sheltered place for the wind's duration is a hummer helper. During Albuquerque's canyon winds I move some feeders to the lee side of my home. When I discovered a hummer taking refuge from a blow among low branches of a cedar sheltered by my porch, I hung a feeder within a foot of the little fellow. He fed there for the day it took winds to subside.

As for feeder height, I suggest well beyond the leap of a house cat. In roadrunner country, place feeders so as not to give an advantage to this hummingbird grabber.

The Calliope has special needs regarding feeder location. For a discussion on feeder placement for this hummingbird, refer to the Calliope information on p. 124.

If you are a first-time hummingbird feeder, for economy reasons, one small three- or four-ounce capacity feeder is an intelligent start. Additional and larger models can be added as your hummer population increases. A couple of good beginning feeders are the egg-shaped 10-ounce Opus #447, or Perkey-Pet 3-ounce "Little Beginner" #214. Next, should we place feeders in the sun, or shade?

With feeders on the east side of my house, the birds reduced feeding trips proportionally to a rising sun's increasing heat. Part of the reason for their reduced feeding could be because hummingbird energy demands drop with rising air temperature. Nevertheless, after my house shaded the feeder, the birds came more often. As a result of that, I suspect hummingbirds have minds of their own about sunshine and shade.

Feeder Formula

An observation as to why hummingbirds swarm more around one feeder than others that are available: I think the favored feeder may offer the best visibility. Where two feeders are nearly side by side, and yet one is predominately favored, I tend to believe that from a hummingbird's viewpoint, the favored feeder offers better visibility. Although the difference may seem tiny to us, remember, these birds live on the edge, and tend to opt for even the slightest advantage.

Feeder Formula

A majority of hummingbird experts recommend a mixture no richer in sugar than four parts water to one part sugar. This ratio produces a solution of 21 percent sucrose, by weight, which is about average for nectar found in most hummingbird flowers. If you're tempted to offer a ratio higher in sugar than four to one, consider this: in hot weather, water is as important to the birds as sugar. If the birds don't get a water balance meeting hot weather requirements, they may buzz off in search of food with a more favorable water content. In temperatures above 90° F, I use a five-to-one water/sugar mixture because it better suits hummingbird metabolism in hot weather. There are two more reasons for a not overly rich sugar mixture. First, there are hints, but as yet no firm proof, that an overrich sugar mixture tends to give the little birds liver problems. Second, there is evidence that suggests too much sugar reduces the hummingbirds' ability to reproduce. The four-to-one (or five-to-one) water/sugar ratio will encourage hummers to return to a feeder more frequently, which increases the opportunities to see these free spirits in action.

Every batch of feeding solution should be stovetop boiled two minutes to retard fermentation. Use a lid to prevent escaping vapors from concentrating the solution. It's not advisable to microwave sugar water, because microwave radiation heats some of the sugar's elements hotter than water's boiling point. This degree of heating causes a breakdown in the sugar molecule, altering its structure (author's conversation with chemists at the University of New Mexico, 1991). Since no study has been made to determine if the sugar's changed structure is good or bad for hummingbirds, it seems sensible, for now, to not microwave sugar water. (I now understand why the sugar glaze on pastries gets so hot so quickly when microwaved.)

Is there a difference between cane and beet sugar? Sucrose in each is the same, but trace elements in the two sugars are different. Studies have shown that differences between these elements have insignificant nutritional effects, so one sugar is as good as the other for feeding hummingbirds. Cool a boiled mixture before offering it to the birds. Surplus sugar water should be refrigerated. Warm temperatures and/or direct sunshine accelerate fermentation and bacteria growth in sugar water; therefore in summer it is critical that feeders be emptied, cleaned, and recharged with fresh solution every two to four days.

Unlike some birds, hummingbirds refrain from taking fermented food. It is almost as if the birds understand that to fly with the precision hummingbird flight requires, they must be clear headed. Natural selection apparently eliminates individuals from the hummingbird gene pool that don't avoid fermented food. When a bird finds a "bad" feeder, it will fly elsewhere for food, and will be suspect of that feeder for quite a while. To avoid fermentation in very hot weather (95° F and above), a feeder's solution should be changed every other day.

Red dye #2 food coloring may be harmful to the birds. Carroll Peabody, founder and former owner-operator of The Mile Hi/ Ramsey Canyon Preserve in southeastern Arizona, tells of his experience with this color additive.

In 1972 Peabody, aided by several biologists, counted over 1,500 hummingbirds visiting his feeders. Peabody was feeding the Ramsey Canyon hummingbirds a mixture containing red dye #2. Over a span of time he found a few dead hummingbirds. Upon dissecting those hummers, he discovered throat and liver tumors. Suspecting the tumors stemmed from red dye #2, Peabody eliminated that coloring from his sugar water mixture. Banning of red dye #2 by the Food and Drug Administration later in 1972 reenforced Peabody's suspicion. However, in 1981 the FDA's decision was reversed. Then, in October of 1990, cosmetics containing the coloring were recalled, on grounds the substance was suspected of having caused cancer. Regarding red dye #2, Mr. Peabody's contention is, if we wish to voluntarily consume the substance, that is our choice, but is it fair to force material with a clouded reputation onto unsuspecting hummingbirds?

The ultimate hummingbird feeding station may be created by placing pieces of fruit that attract fruitflies and gnats near a feeder. Bananas, peaches, apricots, etc., are good insect attractors. With ripe fruit near a feeder, I have watched the little birds alternate between zapping insects on the fly and going sugar water snorkeling. I have also watched them lap juices flowing from the fruits, especially peaches.

Another natural food source for many hummingbirds comes from a relationship with sapsuckers. Where sapsuckers drill into trees, hummingbirds feed on the oozing sap, plus insects the sap attracts. Sap is such an important part of these hummingbirds' diets the little fellows will follow sapsuckers to find their wells. Sapsucker wells also offer good photo opportunities.

Commercially mixed hummingbird preparations often contain preservatives that may be harmful to the birds. Shipment and shelf storage times give bacteria and fungi increased opportunities to multiply in these preparations.

It is not wise to substitute or add honey or artificial sweeteners to hummingbird mixtures. We, and the hummingbirds, are indebted to Dr. Augusto Ruschi, Brazilian naturalist and bird expert, for discovering that a honey-water mixture breeds a fungus that attacks hummingbird tongues, eventually causing a bird's death. As for artificial sweeteners, they have no substantial food value.

Hummingbird Feeders

What makes a good hummingbird feeder? In my view, "good" is one that solves the hummingbird's greatest problem when it is feeding: is an attacker zipping in? By accident, I discovered a feeding device the birds seemed to prefer over any of the variety of feeders I had used.

For photographic purposes I wanted a feeder with a minimum of obstruction between camera and hummingbird. I experimented with many but wasn't satisfied. At a garage sale I bought a hamster water bottle: a bottle with a glass tube about a quarter of an inch in diameter protruding at an angle from a black rubber stopper. It struck me that the thin, glass tube might be the ultimate feeding device for photo purposes.

I filled the hamster water bottle with a clear sugar-water solution and suspended it in place of another feeder. My plan was to give the birds a few days to get used to it.

I was surprised when the hamster bottle was instantly accepted. That feeder became the most popular in my inventory. Wondering why a device that wasn't supposed to be a hummingbird feeder was such a hit, I sat back and studied the birds while they fed from the bottle.

If you've watched hummingbirds feed, you may have noticed they sip a little, back away, hover, sip again, back away, etc. But when they fed from the hamster bottle, this backing-and-forthing didn't occur. My flying experience led to what I believe is a fair explanation.

It appeared the birds flew to-and-fro primarily at feeders with restricted view of the sky. The birds seemed more comfortable at feeders that allowed better visibility, such as pinched-waist models.

Then it dawned on me: for a feeding hummingbird to meet or avoid an attacker, the bird must be able to scan the sky to spot incoming "bogeys." Bulky or big fake flower feeders caused the birds to stop feeding and back out for a look-see, whereas the hamster bottle's single glass tube provided nearly unlimited visibility.

Although the birds didn't to-and-fro at the bottle, they did shift slightly from side to side, while sipping. It appeared the hummingbird was surveying several slices of sky, as if looking out for attackers.

By observing a feeding bird's reactions while it fed I was soon able to sense when it had an incoming "enemy" sighted, long before the enemy had flown over the fence into the yard. It was amusing to watch the feeding hummer keep right on feeding, almost nonchalantly, as the bogey bored on. Often waiting until the last possible second, the feeding bird would spin from the feeder into an eye-popping, tail-standing, pirouetting, squeaking face-off. Invariably the attacker seemed surprised at the feeding bird's sudden spin. Perhaps because its target kept feeding, the attacker felt it was undetected and may have arrived at the feeder feeling it had an easy mark. Regardless, the feeding bird's last-second "Surprise!" face-off usually won, and the attacker had to wait its turn.

When shopping for a feeder, if a hummingbird were with you, I believe it would favor designs that provide good visibility at the moment of feeding. That said, I will continue using all types, sizes, and shapes of feeders because the birds react differently to each kind and I enjoy the variety of their reactions.

There are basically two types of feeders: vacuum principle, which are prone to drip, and pan, also known as basin feeders, which are less likely to drip. Homemade feeders are an option, and they too can be made in the two basic types. There are advantages and disadvantages to each.

All pan (basin) feeders function essentially the same, and all are inherently dripproof. Pan feeders are simply a pan covered by another pan with feeding ports. These feeders are bee and wasp resistant, and most are big bird resistant. On a ranch in southeastern New Mexico that had a population of between six and seven hundred hummingbirds, including four species, the pan feeder was a favorite.

Some pan feeders are fitted with a steel hanger rod from center, ¼″ or smaller, or a small chain. Such a rod or chain is a tiny hindrance to the birds for spotting bogeys or predators. However, if you want to provide the ultimate in visibility, eliminate the rod and mount the feeder on a post. (Post-mounted feeders will invite ants and a variety of animals; therefore ant and animal proofing will be necessary.) You may also eliminate the rod and suspend the feeder by a monofilament line. I've seen no bird-monofilament collision problems, probably because hummingbirds regularly work around spiderwebs when they search for small spiders to eat. Incidentally, the more a feeder design allows hummingbirds an open view, the more we have an open view of hummingbirds.

Winds can slosh liquid from suspended pan feeders, but on a smaller scale than vacuum feeders. Wind effects can be reduced by suspending a large lead fishing weight from the feeder's bottom. Or post mounted, a pan feeder should withstand hurricane-force winds. Pan feeders usually have only two parts, and both parts clean easily. Beware of pan feeders that can't be taken apart. Assembly seams of such feeders are breeding grounds for fungi and bacteria. Such infested feeders might infect hummingbirds or generate unpleasant tastes that will send them elsewhere.

The second hummingbird feeder design, the vacuum principle, is sensitive to air temperature and pressure changes. When these elements vary, such as from cool night to warm daytime, the vacuum in these feeders correspondingly changes, raising or lowering liquid levels. This action "pumps" liquid through the feeder's ports, causing them to drip. Little or no drip occurs, however, when enough hummingbirds are feeding to keep the vacuum system in balance.

Different materials are used in feeder construction. Ceramic feeders are generally difficult to clean. Metals used in feeder construction eventually rust or have coatings or elements that may contaminate a sugar-water solution. All glass, with no plastic parts, is good for the same reasons we use glass in many of our utensils. All glass feeders I know of are either the hamster water bottle (under $3.00), hand-blown models (Fire & Ice, Rifle, CO), or homemade. Some of the best hummingbird feeders I've used are easily made at home from glass jars or bottles. A disadvantage to glass is that it may magnify solar heating that can lead to premature fermenting of sugar water, averted by shading the feeder or changing the liquid a little more often than normal.

Plastics are the most commonly used materials in commercial hummingbird feeders. The type of plastic used affects feeder performance and longevity. Three types of plastic are currently used in hummingbird feeder manufacturing. One is a low-cost, petroleum based plastic known as styrene or butyrate. Feeders made of styrenes or butyrates have an outdoor life expectancy from a few months, in extreme desert heat or mountain (high ultraviolet [UV]) areas, to five years in cooler or lower elevation (low UV) areas. Acrylics and polycarbonates, petroleum based plastics, survive weathering better. A third plastic, one with superior weathering qualities, is cellulose-acetate-butyrate (CAB). CAB is derived from cotton or wood fibers and therefore has a longer outdoor life expectancy (ten to fifteen years) than petroleum based plastics.

Feeders made of low-cost plastic have these disadvantages: they expand and contract at lower temperatures (around 80°), contributing to leakage; they crack easily; they soften at both dishwater and hot summer temperatures, and they deteriorate from weather's effects more rapidly. (I have seen low-cost plastic feeders barely make it through one season of desert heat.) High-grade, more expensive materials not only weather better, they also tolerate dishwashers and/or boiling water, where cheaper styrene or butyrate plastics may melt out-of-shape in boiling water.

Superior types of plastics are used in two feeders that I know of, the Hummingbird Circus (Burd Corporation, Cedaredge, CO), made from CAB, and Droll Yankee (Foster, RI), made from polycarbonates. These two feeders are upscale, and therefore more expensive to buy initially. In the long run, polycarbonate and CAB feeders are probably more economical because they last much longer than feeders made from less expensive materials.

Flower petals preferred by hummingbirds reflect light from the UV end of the color spectrum. Recently it was discovered that hummingbird eyes, and the eyes of some other birds and animals, are tuned to ultraviolet emissions (Waldvogel 1990). Apparently, flowers transmitting UV twinkle for hummingbirds in the same way that neon signs shimmer to us. Physicist Jim Saikin of Tucson, Arizona, points out that you may create UV hotspots on your feeder by outlining its ports with a red fluorescent magic marker (Faber-Castell fluorescent highlight markers are UV producers). Saikin added that other UV reflectors can be made by dipping a ribbon strip of cotton material into laundry blueing or by washing the material in laundry detergent containing whiteners (blueing). Affix a flower-sized bow of treated material to your feeder and/or place some around your property.

Fluorescent orange surveyor's flagging tape is also a UV emitter. On feeders with glass tubes, I discard the yellow bee guard and replace it with a small bow of fluorescent orange surveyor's tape. Removing the yellow reduces the feeder's attraction to bees, while a UV-emitting bow has natural appeal to hummingbirds. Hummingbird attraction via UV may be pursued to its ultimate by using a UV meter to read a flower, such as a trumpet vine. With that reading, create pieces of cotton or magic marker spots matching the flower's level of UV. Since this discovery of UV's attraction to hummingbirds, it is probably only a matter of time before feeder manufacturers incorporate UV enhancers into designs that will boost a feeder's hummingbird drawing power. Gold impregnated glass (red glass) is an excellent UV emitter, and in my experience is irresistible to hummingbirds. Once hummingbirds have found your feeder, UV emitters become less important because the birds remember feeder locations from year to year.

To test the effectiveness of the Webster feeder's red-glass ports (see p. 82), I had a local glassblower recreate a Webster design, but with clear glass feeding ports. Around the mouth of each clear glass port I tied a ribbon of fluorescent orange surveyor's tape.

At the Santa Anita Club de Golf in Guadalajara, Mexico, I set the two feeders at locations a mile apart with equivalent Violet-crowned and Broad-billed hummingbird populations, in January. Then I trained identical automatic cameras on each feeder.

The camera covering the feeder with red-glass ports took 108 pictures in two days. The camera at the clear glass feeder with orange ribbon bows took only six pictures in the same period. I switched feeders, leaving each camera untouched. The camera that had taken six pictures in two days finished 36 exposures in a couple of hours when directed toward the red glass feeder.

This was not a strictly controlled scientific test. But it is an indication that gold-impregnated red glass emits color in a wavelength that attracts hummingbirds. The first backyard hummingbird feeder apparently possessed high-tech (UV) attraction qualities.

To perch or not to perch is a question I haven't resolved regarding feeders with built-in perches. After all, the reason these little creatures are known as hummingbirds is because they feed while hovering on humming wings. My anthropomorphic side sympathizes with the kindness of providing the little flappers with a sit-down lunch. However, my rational side questions the benefits, because for hummingbirds to have a sit-down snack seems unnatural. Biologists say that of the 160 or more native North American flowering plants exclusively pollinated by hummingbirds, not one produces flowers with a sit-down platform. One reason for this is to discourage bees as pollinators in favor of hummingbirds.

Lee Gass, a hummingbird expert at the University of British Columbia in Vancouver, has a different viewpoint on perches.

Hovering, for helicopters or birds, requires maximum energy expenditure (Weis-Fogh 1972). Gass points out that one flower yields a food volume equal to about ¼₀ of a raindrop per hummingbird visit. A flower feeding hummingbird need hover only briefly to deplete the plant's nectar before proceeding forward into easier, translational lift flight. Therefore, in feeding at a flower, the bird's maximum energy expenditure is brief. By contrast, a feeder provides an infinite volume of food per visit. At a feeder, a hummingbird's maximum energy expenditure is prolonged while it tanks up. Prolonged hovering, beyond what is "natural," could tire the bird's flight muscles. From that standpoint, providing a feeder with a perch makes sense. There are additional reasons for perches on some hummingbird feeders.

If you live at an elevation above 6,000 feet, from my experience perches are important. Thin air found at high altitudes is less dense, therefore providing less lift. To understand this air density phenomenon better, consider this: at 15,000 feet in the Andes Mountains of South America lives a hummingbird known as the Andean Hillstar. This hummingbird lives higher than any other hummingbird. At 15,000 feet the air is so thin the Andean Hillstar doesn't hover. Consequently, this hummer feeds at only one species of flower, a flower that has apparently coevolved with this specific hummingbird. During coevolvement, the flower grew structures providing the Andean Hillstar with a perch for the bird's use while taking on nectar (and pollinating). Another reason for perches at high altitudes is that less oxygen found there accelerates the tiring of flight muscles. High in the Rocky Mountains, many hummingbirds clamp onto the feeding port of a feeder that has no perches. Thus clamped, the birds have the posture of a feeding woodpecker. That posture on a hummingbird is, to me, at once pathetic and comical. The little bird seems to simply be making the best of a bad situation. Sometimes even low altitude hummingbirds suffer tired flight muscles and find a perch-equipped feeder useful.

In spring and fall I have seen nearly exhausted migrating hummers flutter to my feeder as if they were barely hanging on. For these weary travelers to sit while they catch their breath, and feed, seems right. One arriving female Black-chinned perched and fed over five minutes, alternating between feeding and resting. On windy days I've seen the little birds clamp onto the perch of a swinging feeder. Hanging on, the bird rocked back and forth with the feeder, while feeding. Further, to see an egg laden female hovering to feed, when her body weight is 10–20 percent greater than normal, is to cast a vote favoring perches. In summer, when young birds are learning to fly, "training perches" seem important through the period it takes little ones to gain full hovering strength. And larger sized hummingbirds may need perches because they expend more energy per unit of time to hover than smaller sized hummingbirds (Hainesworth 1972).

I now hang a combination of feeders with and without perches, giving the birds a choice. One feeder, Hummingbird Circus (Burd Corporation, Cedaredge, CO), is designed to force the birds to perch while feeding. The idea behind the design is that a perched bird is more difficult for a bully to bully. Brown's Hummy-Bird Bar (Hummingbird Haven, Semi Valley, CA) offers a feeder with perches at half its ports and no perches at the other half. Other manufacturers have perches designed to allow the bird to either feed on the wing, or perch and feed. There seems to be more hummingbird action and interplay around feeders that have perches.

An item to remember about most feeders and rain: rainwater may dilute your sugar water solution. The amount of dilution depends on the rain's intensity and the feeder's design. (In Albuquerque after a heavy rain Dave Shivell watched a Black-chinned hummingbird come to his feeder, take one sip, and quickly depart, apparently in search of a sweeter deal.) Many feeder manufacturers offer an optional canopy, good for both rain and sun.

Another consideration in choosing a feeder is that the fewer its parts, the easier it is to clean. Also, you will attract more birds with several small feeders, which equals more hummingbird territories, than with a few large models.

If no commercial feeder suits your needs, you can make your own. I have offered hummingbirds sugar water from a red-topped beef bouillon cube jar with a ⅛" hole in the lid; a miniature coffee cup; a small stainless steel coffee creamer shaped like a pitcher; a sea shell; a jar lid; a miniature root beer mug; a wine glass; etc. Hummingbirds fed, and returned to feed, from each container.

Making your own feeder is easier if you begin with a small bottle that comes with a red cap or lid. Drill a ⅛" hole through the cap's top near its edge and wrap a stiff wire around the jar below the cap. Leave a loop for hanging and fill with sugar water. The liquid level must be kept high in order for the hummingbird to reach it through the cap. If you have a lot of birds, you'll have to top the liquid frequently. This homemade feeder design is a pan type, and therefore won't drip from weather changes. Hail damage and rain dilution should be minor, and with only two parts it is easy to clean.

An excellent homemade vacuum feeder can be made from an

8-ounce mayonnaise or salad dressing jar. I have made several, and find them superior to commercial models because they clean easily and are dishwasher safe, provide hummingbirds good sky visibility, have no rain dilution, and have years of durability. Here are materials needed to make this feeder:

One 8-oz. mayonnaise or salad dressing jar.

One rubber laboratory stopper size 10½ (between $2 and $2.50).

A 3-inch piece of 8mm glass tubing (must be precisely three inches).

A couple of wire coathangers *or* 4½ feet of #14 green insulated solid copper wire.

To make the feeder:

Freeze the laboratory stopper and drill a hole $^{19}/_{64}$ inch a little off-center (use glycerine or liquid soap for drilling lubricant).

Heat glass tubing with a propane torch about ¾ inch from one end. Bend tubing approximately 30 degrees. Bend *must not kink,* as liquid won't flow properly. Insert short end of glass tube into hole in stopper.

Surround the bottle with a cradle fashioned from either a coathanger or #14 insulated solid copper wire. Suspend a filled bottle so that its mouth hangs 20–25 degrees downward. Tie fluorescent bow of orange surveyor's tape near tip of glass tubing.

Care and Cleaning of Feeders

It is important that feeders be washed with a bottle brush and rinsed well before refilling. Detergents for feeder cleaning break down water's surface tension. If a feeder isn't completely purged, detergent residue will continue to break surface tension and will encourage leakage from vacuum-principle feeders. White vinegar and water is a good detergent substitute. Another successful cleaning method is to soak a disassembled feeder 15 minutes in a solution of ½ cup liquid bleach diluted by 2 quarts of water, followed by a thorough rinse. At the University of British Columbia, biologist Lee Gass soaks feeders in a weak bleach solution every other day for 24 hours, followed by a good rinse. For tough cleaning jobs, a little sand and/or gravel in saltwater agitated in a feeder may help. Denture cleaners are an effective feeder cleanser, but thorough rinsing is critical.

Unfortunately, the sweet mixture used to attract hummingbirds also attracts bees, wasps, ants, bigger birds, raccoons, and in the southwest, bats and bears. There are methods to restrain each of these uninvited guests.

Surveyor's tape on tubing.

Controlling Uninvited Guests at Feeders

As for bigger birds at hummingbird feeders, providing them with their own seed or nectar feeders helps. Personally, I enjoy watching an oriole acting like a hummingbird at a feeder. I also like the oriole's appetite for tent caterpillars and other "harmful" insects. For other large birds that insist on visiting hummingbird feeders, the only acceptable solution I know is a "bird proof" feeder sold by several firms. Insects are a different problem.

Mother Nature, in her wisdom, has attempted to give plant pollinators—bees, butterflies, and hummingbirds—separate departments of flowers. She did this through corolla shape and colorization: yellows, with higher sucrose and higher fragrance, for bees and butterflies; reds and shades of red, with less sucrose, and lower fragrance, for hummingbirds.

Yellow plastic flower shapes and/or yellow bee guards are a color attractant for butterflies and bees. Since this information surfaced,

69

some manufacturers offer red replacement flowers and bee guards. Removing the yellow parts from a feeder and discarding them is another solution, or paint them with red nail polish. Unfortunately, bees and wasps that visited a feeder with yellow parts will continue. There is a solution.

A vacuum cleaner can be used to vacuum insects off the feeder. After five to ten wasps are taken, and about the same number of bees, feeders should be relatively clear of these insects for the summer. (Apologies to the world's wasps, bees, and beekeepers.) Wasps will not reappear for a long time because they are territorial; after a number are "neutralized," the territory they claimed is empty, until newcomers move in.

Early control of wasps is important, otherwise wasp parents *and* offspring will crowd feeders by late summer. Remington offers a cordless Bug Sucker that appears capable of the vacuuming job. Also, some bird feeder firms offer a wasp trap. If bees continue to be a problem after vacuuming, the problem may be with the sugar solution being poured into the feeder.

As mentioned earlier, the overall average sucrose content of hummingbird flowers is 21 percent, which is how we arrived at the four-to-one water-sugar mixture. Mother Nature has generally reserved flowers with nectar richer in sucrose for bees and butterflies. When bees find a feeder containing a sucrose mixture rich enough to suit their taste, they fly to the hive and do a spinning dance with wiggles and waggles to tell fellow bees the way to a feeder that is extra sweet. From then on, that hummingbird feeder becomes a bee feeder. To reduce bees at a feeder, replace its yellow parts and keep sugar solutions at one part sugar to four parts water. If bees continue to be a problem, thin your mixture to one part sugar and five parts water until the bees give up and leave. This mixture almost always eliminates bees while retaining hummingbirds. The birds stay with a five-to-one mix because that is a sucrose content well within the limit of hummingbird flowers. (Since bees collect nectar from flowers that are nature's highest sucrose producers, I now understand why honey can be substituted in cooking recipes at about half the amount called for in sugar.)

Even after you've done it all correctly, in lean yellow flower years, and in the fall when flowers are diminishing, bees may visit all red feeders, even those with a sucrose content of five to one. Vacuuming remains an alternative. Ants require a different approach.

Soon after your feeder is up, chances are it will be found by ants. After all, ants have been successful foragers for 130 million years. Ants on a hummingbird's tongue, or in a hummingbird's throat, can't be outflown or outmaneuvered. Hummingbirds that find a feeder with ants usually stop visiting and may not return for a long time. Fortunately there is an easy way to foil ants.

A water moat can be fashioned from a 5-ounce Vienna sausage (or similar) can sandwiched between a ³⁄₁₆″ turnbuckle, two washers, and two "O" rings. Suspend this device between anchor point and feeder. Fill the can with water. Although ants have been around a long time, they haven't learned to swim. The sooner you install a moat above your feeder, the sooner your hummingbird investment will be protected. There is another ant control method. Although it is quick and easy, it isn't as clean as a water moat.

Kay Cooper of Cedar Crest, New Mexico, has found that shortening, such as Crisco, applied to a feeder's suspension wire stops ants.

Bats, especially in the southwest, can also be a problem at feeders. There are at least three species of nectar-feeding bats: the Mexican long-nosed (formerly known as Sanborn's long-nosed bat); the lesser (little) long-nosed (*Sanborni*); and in southern California, southern Arizona, southwestern New Mexico, the area around Big Bend, Texas, and nearly all of Mexico, the Mexican long-tongued bat (*Cheronycteris mexicana* Tschudi).

The Mexican long-tongued bat commonly feeds at hummingbird feeders during the night. These night-flying mammals are equipped with an acute sense of smell, tuned to home in on sucrose. A hint that bats may be drinking at hummingbird feeders is finding the containers surprisingly low or empty at morning. One September, when I was filming in Madera Canyon, Arizona, it was common for Mexican long-tongues to empty every feeder during the night. See p. 73 for the range of this bat. Note the animal's range coincides with the hummingbird belt of southern California, Arizona, and part of New Mexico. Some of these bats are on endangered species lists (Endangered Species Update, 1990). The good side is, these little night flyers eat many insects, and are probably well worth feeding. I think so highly of bats because of the approximately 2,000 mosquitoes per night each bat consumes. I have encouraged them to coexist with "my" hummingbirds by providing them with a bat house. (For bat house plans, check with Dr. Merlin D. Tuttle, Bat Conservation International, c/o Milwaukee Public Museum, Milwaukee, Wisconsin 53233). However, if you live in a bat area, and aren't interested in feeding bats, the only solution I know is to take feeders in at night, or use feeders with bee (bat) guards. Considering that hummingbirds

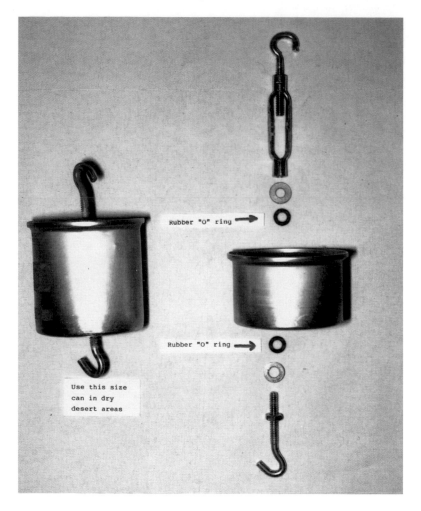

Feeder with moat.

begin feeding as early as twenty minutes before sunrise, taking feeders in is an inconvenient solution. To make matters worse, nectar-feeding bats may remember feeder locations from one year to the next . . . an advantage if you feed them. Bears around feeders, however, are seldom an advantage, except for feeder manufacturers.

It is no secret that bears like sweets. In Portal, Arizona, Russ Griffiths, operator of the Portal store, told me of the night he was roused in response to a commotion in his yard. Armed with a small .22 caliber rifle loaded with bird shot that could do little more than sting, Griffiths expected to find javelina rooting in his flower beds. To his surprise the clamor was caused by a black bear slurping at the Griffiths' hummingbird feeders. The bear made off with one feeder that has

Bat at Hummingbird feeder

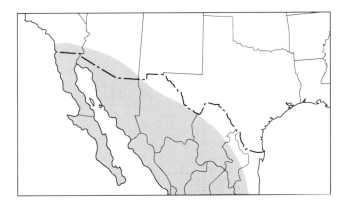

Distribution of the Cheronycteris mexicana bat in Northern Mexico.

never been found. One August evening while I was filming humming-birds during their sundown feeding frenzy at the 120-year-old log headquarters house of Cooper Ranch in the Sandia Mountains next to Albuquerque, a black bear strolled into the yard. The animal sniffed the air until he tracked the sugar water. When he found the scent, he proceeded to raid four one-quart feeders, scattering hummingbirds and feeder pieces. I missed this bear photo opportunity because my cameras were locked on a hummingbird filming stage.

When food conditions are poor on the bear's natural feeding grounds, the animals may also raid hummingbird feeders in broad daylight. A good response is to hang feeders up out of reach of these animals. Out of reach for southwestern bears is above ten feet. With proper respect for the bear's strength and unpredictability, such an event offers a bear photo opportunity.

Taming the Rufous Hummingbird

In an RV park in Kino Bay, Sonora, Mexico I met a retiree so enraged at Rufous hummingbirds taking over his feeders from other hummers at his Texas home, he simply shot all Rufous birds. Shabby treatment, I thought, for any creature, but especially shabby for the Rufous, a hummer I consider to be the world's greatest hummingbird. There is a rational way to tame the Rufous.

Understanding what makes Rufous hummingbirds tick allows us to manipulate their dominating behavior. First, Rufous humming-birds are known as "generalist" feeders, as opposed to "trapline" feed-ers. As you might suspect, generalist feeders tend to forage over a specific area, whereas trapliners tend to forage by cruising along a par-ticular route each day. Second, Rufous hummingbirds favor areas with flowers richer in nectar. And, if you've seen Rufous hummingbirds in action, you know how adept this hummingbird is at defending a nectar source it wants. Add to that mix the fact that one feeder is the equivalent of 2,000 to 5,000 flowers worth of nectar, per day. It should be clear why this little bird tends to take over feeders. But keep in mind, those habits make him easy to manipulate. An additional clue to controlling Rufous birds comes from the century plant, a Rufous favorite.

Blooming century plants are generally spaced far enough apart so that one Rufous can defend only one plant. The flowers of these plants range from eight to fifteen feet high. Invariably a Rufous who has staked out a century plant perches either at the top of his "property", or very near its top. An *area* with *rich* nectar that is eight to fifteen feet *high* can be used to tame this little hummingbird.

When the first Rufous migrants arrive in Albuquerque and jostle Black-chins, Broad-tails, and Calliopes for feeder possession, I suspend a feeder twelve feet high at a corner of my home. Next, I fill the high feeder with a three-and-a-half-to-one water-sugar solution—slightly richer than four to one. For the other hummingbirds, I place feeders no higher than six feet and no nearer than fifteen feet to the elevated, nectar-rich feeder. These lower feeders I fill with a four-and-a-half-to-one water-sugar solution—weaker than a normal four to one.

The Rufous, being what he is, sampled the nectar in all of the feeders. After he discovered the highest feeder contained the richest nectar, he took over that feeder. Between feedings he perched on a nail suspending the feeder, hour after hour, even in hot sun. In other words, the Rufous bird behaved toward the higher, richer feeder as he does when occupying a century plant. Although other hummingbirds occasionally rose toward Mr. Rufous, if the incoming bird tracked in a way that was not directly toward the high feeder, Mr. Rufous simply sat and watched. However, if the intruder's track projected within three to five feet of the high feeder, Mr. Rufous launched and defended his territory in typical, winning, Rufous style. Every now and then the Rufous would launch, scatter the "common" hummingbirds from their lower feeders, and sample their nectar. Invariably the Rufous returned to his feeder without making an effort to own any of the lower feeding stations. For each male Rufous that appears I install a high, richer-in-nectar feeder. This strategy has created peace among hummingbirds feeding in my back yard.

To accommodate Calliopes, I add a couple of feeders three feet or less above the ground, since that is this bird's niche. With such a system in place, a tri-level guild of more or less harmonious hummingbirds feed at levels natural to each species. Occasional encounters between the birds still occur, but the encounters are minor compared to before. (My Texas friend has promised to give the system a try.)

History of Hummingbird Feeders

In the course of writing this work a question arose: who first had the idea of feeding hummingbirds? The earliest reference I found of a person making an observation about hummingbird feeding was John J. Audubon. In *The Birds of America*, 1840–1844, Vol. IV, page 193, Audubon writes of the Ruby-throated hummingbird, "I have seen many of these birds kept in partial confinement, when they were supplied with artifical flowers . . . in the corollas of which water with honey or sugar dissolved in it was placed." Audubon went on to say these birds "seldom lived many months, while others supplied with fresh flowers and live insects lived 12 months."

Since Audubon makes no mention of feeding hummingbirds himself, and names no one, we are left to speculate who was feeding the hummingbirds. Fifty-five years later, in 1899, Dr. Clifton F. Hodge of Clark University in Worcester, Massachusetts, was more specific. In the October 1899 issue of *Bird-Lore*, the official publication of the Audubon societies, Dr. Hodge wrote an article entitled "A Pleasant Acquaintance with a Hummingbird."

The article begins with Dr. Hodge stating the curriculum of a summer school class he taught that included a section on the honeybee. In Professor Hodge's words,

> The closing laboratory exercise consisted of a 'honey spread,' the honey being removed from the glass hive in the window of the laboratory, in the presence of the class, and distributed with hot biscuits and butter, cream and fresh milk. The spread was pronounced the most enjoyable 'lab work' ever done by the members of the class, but to crown the event in the most exquisite way possible, a Hummingbird flew into an open window, and darting, unafraid, in and out among the noisy groups of fifty or more busy people, it rifled the various flowers with which the laboratory was decorated. In closing the windows for the night it was accidentally imprisoned, and on visiting the room next morning (Sunday), I found it still humming about the flowers. Thinking that it might be a female, with nestlings awaiting its return, I gently placed an insect net over it with the intention of passing it out of the window. It proved, however, on closer inspection, to be a young male, so I thought it could do no harm to keep it a day or two for acquaintance sake. No sooner was my finger, with a drop of honey on it, brought within reach, than it thrust its bill and long tongue out through the net and licked up the honey from my finger with evident delight. Releasing it from the net, I dropped honey into a number of the flowers, sprinkling water over them at the same time, and it immediately began feasting and drinking. As it flew about it taught me its bright little chirp, evidently a note of delight and satisfaction. When I visited the laboratory again at noon, I took in my hand a few heads of red clover and a nasturtium with its horn filled with honey. On giving the chirp a few times, it flew straight to the flowers in my hand, probed each clover tube, drank its fill from the nasturtium, and, perching contentedly on my finger, wiped its bill, preened its feathers, spread out its tail, scratched its head, and for the space of a minute or two looked me over and made himself the most delightful of tiny friends.
>
> The next time I entered the room, about two hours later, he flew to the door to meet me, and this time I took him home, the better to care for him during the afternoon and evening. In the course of the afternoon about a dozen friends

called. Each one was provided with a nasturtium into which a drop of honey
had been placed, and nearly the whole time the little bird was flying from one
to the other, perching on fingers or sipping from the flowers held in the hand or
buttonhole, to the delight of everybody, none of the company having ever seen
a live Hummingbird so close.

Dr. Hodge continues his account by describing how, at sundown,
the hummingbird "went to roost high up on a chandelier. When we
tried to catch the little bird to place it in a cage, he fell like a dead bird
to the carpet."

Apparently the phenomenon of hummingbirds going into torpor
was unknown in 1899. Dr. Hodge continues, "I held him warm in my
hand, thinking that he was about to breathe his last, but anxious to
save the precious little life if possible, I very gently opened the bill and
inserted a pellet of crushed spiders' eggs as large as a good sized sweet
pea, following it with a drop of water. After a moment, the little bird
quit feigning, as they are known to do, and in a minute was bright
and lively as ever."

It seems reasonable to assume that the warmth of Dr. Hodge's
hand brought the bird out of torpor, and the hummer, in Professor
Hodge's words, "quit feigning."

Next morning, when Dr. Hodge went to class, he took the bird in
a cage. In class he placed two fresh nasturtiums in his buttonhole, "one
well loaded with honey, the other filled with the juices of crushed
spiders and spiders' eggs." When Hodge released the hummingbird,
"the little charmer was probing the buttonhole flowers. Then, as if
anxious to show off, he again perched on my hand and went through
his *post prandial* toilet. Some said that I must be in league with higher
powers, and it all must have been 'providential.' This may be true, for
anything I know to the contrary. But it may have been simply improv-
ing the opportunities of a happy accident; and 'accidents,' we know,
'never happen among the Hottentots.' If flowers and honey can do it,
at any rate, such accidents shall be more frequent about my home in
the future."

This biology professor teaching about honeybees discovered the
effects of offering a sweet mixture to a hummingbird. If we take the
schoolmaster at his word, we must assume that following his "happy
accident," Dr. Hodge fed other hummingbirds around his home by
again introducing honey and water and spider eggs and juices into the
horns of nasturtiums. In my mind, that makes Dr. Hodge the first
documented person to feed hummingbirds. A year after the profes-

sor's "Pleasant Acquaintance With a Hummingbird," a lady devised what historically may be the first artificial feeder.

In Brookline, Massachusetts, 36 miles from Clark University, Miss Caroline G. Soule wrote for the October 1900 *Bird-Lore*, "One day I painted a trumpet flower in water-colors on a rather stiff piece of Whatman paper. I painted it as a real flower would look if slit down on one side and spread flat, and I colored both sides. Then I cut out the flower, bent it into shape, and fastened the edges together. Inside the tube I put a small, cylindrical bottle, and tied the flower to the trumpet creeper in an almost normal position. The little bottle I filled with sugared-water, not too thick.

"To my delight the Hummingbird visited that flower with no more hesitation than the real ones, and very soon preferred it, and I had to fill up the bottle at least twice a day."

Within Miss Soule's article she refers to the hummingbird as *she*. Because the Ruby-throated is the only commonly reported hummingbird in Massachusetts, (there has been a single confirmed sighting of an Allen's, and a few Rufous) we must assume that the first hummingbird feeder customer was a female Ruby-throated.

After reading Miss Soule's account, I wrote the university and asked if their records showed her to have been a student there in 1899, and if so, was she a student of Professor Hodge during the time of the hummingbird incident. The university's historical registrar, Stuart Campbell, reported that Clark was not coeducational in 1899. Campbell added that in the summer sessions, occasionally female teachers were allowed to attend. Unfortunately, attendance records for those summer classes were informal, dependent on whether a student signed into a specific class. If Miss Soule was a summer student, she chose not to sign because records don't show her name. That Professor Hodge published his hummingbird experience in *Bird-Lore*, and a year later Miss Soule, living near Clark University, wrote her hummingbird experience in *Bird-Lore*, hints that Miss Soule may have read Professor Hodge's account. Or she may have heard about it, or possibly read of it in a newspaper account, and then carried his lapel flower experiment a step farther. Or, she may have figured out hummingbird feeding on her own. Either way, we must credit Miss Soule's use of a glass bottle with advancing the concept of backyard hummingbird feeding.

The next account of hummingbird feeding, in 1907, is Althea R. Sherman's "Experiments in Feeding Hummingbirds During Seven Summers." Ms. Sherman lived in National, Iowa, and published her work in *The Wilson Bulletin*, December 1913.

History of Hummingbird Feeders

In 1907 Ms. Sherman fed Ruby-throated hummingbirds. She contributed to our knowledge by discovering, among other things, that the bird's behavior can be modified. Ms. Sherman discovered that in time, hummingbirds will come to plain, unadorned feeding bottles filled with clear liquid. Her experiments proved that the birds recognized the bottles simply as food containers. (I successfully duplicated Ms. Sherman's feeding method, using small plastic vials.) Ms. Sherman also observed that in the spring, newly arriving Ruby-throats flew to and hovered at precise spots where feeding bottles had been the previous year. Ms. Sherman estimated that each Ruby-throated consumed one teaspoon of sugar per day. From that observation, she calculated that if human adults required food at this rate, the average person would eat nearly three hundred pounds of sugar a day.

After Ms. Sherman's 1913 publication of her experience, there is little doubt in my mind that many people began backyard feeding of hummingbirds from small bottles. Margaret L. Bodine of Philadelphia, in a June 1928 *National Geographic* article, wrote of her hummingbird feeding experience at a summer home called Birdbank in Asticou, near Northeast Harbor, Maine. "Our [clematis] flowers are not the secret of our porch's attraction for them, but miniature bottles, about two inches long, covered with some bright-hued material and filled with sugared water." Miss Bodine arrived at a sugar-water mixture by tasting flower nectar and matching the nectar's taste to that of her mixture.

"Those bottles are fastened among the blossoms and are speedily discovered by the Humming Birds. Once found, there are few daylight hours from the middle of June 'til September when at least one is not there. Sometimes as many as eight are feasting at a time. One was quite an acrobat, clinging to the bottle with its feet and bracing itself with its tail while it drank. Another, one we called 'Crazy Jane' because she invariably drank off the outside of the bottle near its bottom, where overflow sugar and water ran down; never from the top, as would the average bird."

Small bottles were a big step toward the development of a true hummingbird feeder. Another step in that direction came from Robert S. Woods of Azusa, California.

In July 1929, Woods created an artificial hummingbird feeder from "a four ounce dark bottle with a diagonal hole through the cork" (Woods 1931). The bottle was suspended on its side and angled slightly downward. Woods called this device a hummingbird "filling station." He described it as: "well suited to the hummingbird's convenience."

Woods also experimented with "an automatic drinking fountain formed by inverting a bottle into a small cup." This vacuum-principle feeder was called by Woods, "a bee-proof [hummingbird] drinking fountain." Of this feeder, he points out that "the solution is held at a constant level as long as liquid remains in the inverted bottle." In other words, Woods' feeder was automatic. He equipped both of his hummingbird feeding devices with perches.

These two hummingbird feeder designs were another step toward a backyard feeder. However, Woods had created his feeders for use in an experiment to test Anna's hummingbirds' sense of smell, and as a sideline to see if the birds could be lured to his yard. His intention wasn't to become involved with the regular feeding of humming-birds. He added, "Superior types of feeding devices could of course easily be designed, but it was the intention (for the experiment) to use materials and methods which might come readily to hand."

Although Woods was on the brink of inventing a true backyard feeder, we can only guess that he didn't pursue "superior types" be-cause his interests were in other directions and apparently he didn't recognize the potential of a backyard feeder.

In 1936 an article, "Feeding Hummingbirds in California," by B.F. Tucker, appeared in the July-August issue of *Bird-Lore*. Writing from his weekend home in the foothills between Los Angeles and San Diego, Tucker stated, "Early in 1927 I put out three small test tubes, attaching them to trees by wire arms about three feet long. To attract the birds, I tied brightly colored ribbons to the tubes, then filled them with honey. It took about two weeks for the hummers to decide to test this new plant. Thereafter they became regular feeders."

Tucker goes on to say that by 1930 his hummingbird population had increased to the point where the birds ate so much, he couldn't keep test tubes filled with enough liquid to last one weekend to the next. "I need more and larger feeding devices, [so] I devised an auto-matic feeder, consisting of a quart container with a narrow neck (a flask) inverted into a wide bottomed glass (such as a whisky sour glass) about two inches deep."

Tucker's hummingbird population soon required twenty-five of these quart feeders. He placed them in a row on an ant-proofed 2×4 and called the feeding station his hummingbird bar. To discourage bees, (bees are to be expected with a honey offering) Tucker covered the bottom glass portion of his feeders with a doughnut shaped piece of sheet metal perforated with eight feeding holes. That created two hundred feeding places. Later he installed a wire rail about the bottom glass, hoping to give the hummingbirds a place to perch while they fed. Tucker said of his perch offering, "While skeptical at first, the birds soon learned to clamp their tiny claws around the wire and sit to eat."

Tucker's flask inverted into an upright glass with a perch was based on the same principle as Woods' "bee-proof drinking fountain." The historical difference in these two feeders was that Tucker's main aim was to feed hummingbirds. Feeding hummingbirds received wider publicity than Woods' experiment in determining a hummingbird's sense of smell.

Tucker's reference to his feeder being automatic meant that as liquid level in the wide bottom glass lowered, atmospheric pressure caused liquid in the storage flask to transfer to the bottom glass, constantly balancing inner outer air pressures, thus automatically maintaining a level supply in the glass. Woods' design performed in exactly the same manner, and this same physical law is applied in the design of today's vacuum-principle feeder. (Tucker said his flask-glass combination was an adaptation from a vacuum-principle watering device used for farmyard chickens.)

In 1939 Tucker's mountain home was donated to the California Audubon Society. Formerly known as the Dorothy May Tucker Bird Sanctuary, it is now the Tucker Wildlife Sanctuary. This preserve is owned by California State University, Fullerton Foundation, and is a non-profit organization. The sanctuary is located 16 miles east of Orange.

The Woods and Tucker feeders were the first real hummingbird feeders I have been able to uncover. Certainly they were an improvement over small bottles and test tubes. Unfortunately, the size of Tucker's feeder placed it beyond the scope of a backyard urban feeder. The development of a true backyard hummingbird feeder was destined to come out of New Hampshire, via Cambridge, Massachusetts, between 1929 and 1935. However, that feeder wouldn't reach the public's attention until August of 1947.

Small bottles continued to be used for backyard feeding for more than a decade. In 1936, Roger Tory Peterson wrote in Leaflet No. 56 of the National Association of the Audubon Society, "Make a hummingbird cafeteria. Take some small glass bottles or vials and wrap ribbon or crepe around them so they will resemble flowers. Fill these with sugar water and place them in the garden or someplace around the school grounds where hummingbirds might find them."

Peterson's small bottle suggestion was most likely aimed at using bottles recycled from a previous use, such as pills. The first advertisement I found for hummingbird bottles was in the January 1947 *Audubon* magazine. The National Audubon Society advertised a small bottle described for hummingbird feeding. The caption under a drawing of the bottle read, "Three for $1.50, boxed; two jumbo for $1.50." In the midyear issue of that magazine, Bruce Kelly of South Bend, Indiana, advertised the same bottle, using the same drawing. Both the Kelly ad and the Audubon ads continued into 1950. The genuine urban backyard hummingbird feeder that was designed between 1929 and 1935 was about to become known worldwide after years of obscurity.

In Boston, Mr. and Mrs. Laurence J. Webster read Margaret Bodine's 1928 *National Geographic* account of attracting hummingbirds with small bottles and sugar water. The piece prompted Mrs. Webster to begin feeding hummingbirds in the same manner at their summer home on a lake in Holderness, New Hampshire. The Websters' hummingbird feeding led to two historical events: Harold Edgerton's photographing hummingbirds for the first time with his revolutionary strobe photo flash invention, and Mr. Webster's designing the first truly appropriate backyard hummingbird feeder.

Mrs. Webster suffered from a long-term illness. She took comfort in feeding Ruby-throated hummingbirds, using her empty pill bottles as feeders at their summer retreat. Mrs. Webster's Ruby-throated population grew. Her husband noted that it was a demanding task for his wife to keep the little bottles filled with hummingbird liquid. Using his engineering background, he drew plans for a hummingbird feeding device to be made entirely of hand-blown glass.

Webster took a drawing of his feeder to the glass-blowing lab serving the chemistry and physics departments of his alma mater, the Massachusetts Institute of Technology in Cambridge. Sometime between 1929 and 1935, the unique device was created from a 5 inch section of glass tubing 1¼ inch in diameter. The bottom of the feeder was reduced in diameter and two opposing upcurving ports, formed from ½ inch glass tubing, were affixed. Near the feeder's middle, a slight bulge was formed. An eye for hanging topped the device. After experimenting with various colors for feeding-port tubing, Webster settled on gold-impregnated (red) glass.

MIT records list one glassblower, James (Jimmy) Ryan, in MIT phone directories between 1930 and 1935. I sent a photo of the Webster feeder to Jimmy Ryan's son Lawrence, a retired glassblower living in Daytona Beach, Florida. Lawrence Ryan wrote, "My dad was famous for his ability to fabricate novelty ware in addition to his scientific glassblowing. It is entirely possible that he may have blown the bird feeder."

I also sent a photo of the feeder to Harold Edgerton's widow, Esther, in Cambridge, Massachusetts. Mrs. Edgerton wrote, "I remember seeing several of the feeders. As for the glass blower, the name Jim Ryan sounds familiar."

I also sent a photo of the Webster feeder to Roger Tory Peterson, seeking his recollection of early hummingbird feeders. Peterson wrote, "I cannot remember [for certain] when I saw my first real hummingbird feeder. It could have been at Mr. Tucker's home in California in the late thirties . . . when I was lecturing for Audubon."

For more information about Webster's feeder I talked with his daughter-in-law, Helen Trik of Santa Fe. Ms. Trik said around thirty of the feeders were made for Mrs. Webster's use sometime between 1929 and 1935. She recalls that soon after the feeders were made, hummingbird feeding became a social event at the Websters' home. People from Holderness and surrounding towns were allowed free access to the Webster grounds Sunday afternoons, after church, to see hummingbirds. Ms. Trik said that for this event, feeders were placed throughout the ground's formal gardens and along the home's long porches. For many years, New England socializing was woven into Ruby-throated hummingbird watching at the Websters'.

Since hummingbird feeding was uncommon when Webster created his feeder, sale of the item wasn't his intention. However, Edgerton's 1947 *National Geographic* article, about his strobe flash, presented photos of hummingbirds feeding at Webster's feeder. The piece generated at least one known request for purchase of the device.

In Pine Bluff, Arkansas, ten-year-old William Shepherd was feeding hummingbirds from bottles. Shepherd, now living in Little Rock, remembers showing the *Geographic* article to his father. Young Shepherd's father wrote Webster, asking where the feeder Edgerton used to attract hummingbirds for his photos could be bought. Webster gave Shepherd's father an address and he ordered three of the Webster feeders.

Considering the wide circulation of *National Geographic*, it seems plausible that other readers contacted Webster with purchase requests. Those sales may have been the first for a backyard hummingbird feeder; the Webster Hanging Feeder.

Laurence Webster, Jr., found one of his grandfather's MIT feeders

Hummers feeding at Webster feeder.

in attic storage in New Hampshire and sent it to me. The Webster feeder is a one-piece device relying on the vacuum principle. The design is ingenious. From the photo above we can see today's New Mexico Black-chins enjoying that Webster feeder as much as New Hampshire's Ruby-throats did over half a century ago.

Three years after Edgerton's hummingbird article appeared, the Webster feeder was offered for sale by Audubon's mail order gift shop. The feeder was simply called the Webster Feeder and sold for $3.00. It had taken between sixteen and twenty-one years for the feeder Laurence Webster had designed for his wife's use to become known. And with Audubon's 1950 advertisement, the day of the commercial backyard hummingbird feeder dawned.

In 1951 what may have been the second commercial feeder was a patented device named the Audubon. This vacuum-principle feeder was designed around a modified test tube with a fake flower at its feeding port. Today's Perky-Pet "Little Beginner" model is similar to the 1951 "Audubon." The "Audubon" was offered by the Audubon Novelty Company of Medina, N.Y.

Brown's Hummy-Bird Bar, originally of Tejunga, California, was also an early commercial feeder. This feeder, designed in 1955, was still on the market in 1992. Around 1960, a hand-blown glass feeder based on Webster's design was sold from San Antonio, Texas. Called Dinah Dee's Fabulous Hummingbird Feeder, it cost $1.95. By the spring of 1967 there were at least five commercial hummingbird feeders advertised in *Audubon* magazine.

In the mid 1960s an impressive feeder was based on a glass half-pint cream bottle, the type used before paper cartons. The bottle's black rubber stopper was a science lab type. Glass tubing projected from a hole in the stopper and bent upward to form a single feeding port. Coathanger wire cradled the bottle. The wire served as a hanger and a perch. This cream bottle design was made at Hummingbird Corners. The feeders sold for "a couple of bucks." I have one of these cream bottle feeders and find it excellent.

During the 1970s many new hummingbird feeder designs appeared. Strangely enough, however, it wasn't until 1981 that a hummingbird feeder manufacturer (Perky-Pet Products, Inc.,) first advertised and was classified in *Thomas' Register of Manufacturers*. Today, hummingbird feeder manufacturing is considered a growth industry.

Feeder Manufacturers

Aspects Inc., Box 408, Warren, RI 02885
Briggs Associates Inc., Box 29310, Thornton, CO 80229
Brown Co., Narragansett, RI 02882
Burd Corp., Box 580, Cedaredge, CO 81413-0580 (CAB plastic)
Crystal Ridge Feeders, Box 1300, Julian, CA 92036
Droll Yankee, 27 Mill Rd., Foster, RI 02825 (Polycarbonate plastic)
Duncraft, 33 Fisherville Rd., Penacook, NH 03303
Fire & Ice Glass, Box 983, Rifle, CO 81650 (All glass)
Heath Mfg. Co., 140 Mill Street, Coopersville, MI 49404
Hummingbird Haven, 1255 Carmel Dr., Simi Valley, CA 93065
Hyde Bird Feeder Co., Box 168, Waltham, MA 02254
North States Industries, Inc., 1200 Mendelssohn Ave., Suite 210, Minneapolis, MN 55427
Opus, Box 525, Bellingham, MA 02019
Penn Pak, Inc., Box 290, Madison, GA 30650

Feeding Hummingbirds

Perky-Pet Products, Inc. 2201 S. Wabash St., Denver, CO 80231
Presto Galaxy, Inc., 255 Banker St., Greenpoint, NY 11222
Pyro's Pottery, 1588 North Sewell Rd., Bloomington, IN 47408
Wildlife Products, Box 363, Wisconsin Rapids, WI 54494
Hamster water bottle: Rolf C. Hagen Corp., Mansfield, MA 02048

Hummingbird Feeding: Good or Bad for the Birds?

Enjoyable as hummingbird feeding can be for us, what about the hummingbirds? Are there long-term physiological effects, good or bad, we are imposing on the hummingbird population? For answers I talked with Bill Baltosser, hummingbird expert at the University of Arkansas; Lee Gass, biologist, hummingbird and physiological ecology expert at the University of British Columbia in Vancouver, Canada; and F. Reed Hainsworth, professor at Syracuse University's Laboratory of Comparative Physiology and Behavior.

Baltosser states, "Man has had a negative impact on many species. But so far, our artificial feeding of hummingbirds apparently has been and is good for the hummingbird, provided feeders are cleaned regularly and filled with proper sugar-to-water ratios without preservatives or food colorings."

F. Reed Hainsworth reasons that as long as we mix sugar and water resulting in a sucrose ratio near the birds' natural diet, the birds probably benefit. He feels that long-term effects on the birds should be little different for birds visiting feeders versus flowers. Hainsworth also believes there are many more hummingbirds because of the ready supply of food from feeders.

Gass, in Canada, says, "Over the last twenty-five years the ranges of hummingbird species have steadily spread northward. It is likely these range increases are due, at least in part, to urban garden hummingbird feeders." Gass contends if that is so, then humans have been good for hummingbirds. He also points out, "It is fortunate that cane (and beet) sugar sucrose and flower sucrose are so nearly identical . . . a happy coincidence for hummingbirds." At the same time Gass is concerned that "urban feeder wars" waged by humans could undo the good.

An urban feeder war exists where one person, in hopes of luring neighboring birds, raises the sugar ratio in his feeders beyond the sucrose percentage found in hummingbird flowers. Hummingbirds, obviously, are caught in the crossfire. Gass is concerned that where this type of feeding is practiced, hummingbird populations may suffer. "As long as urban hummingbird feeding is done responsibly, the birds' lives should benefit."

Proof that hummingbirds use their own heads about visiting backyard feeders comes from the Rocky Mountain Biological Laboratory near Gothic, Colorado. There it was noted that when hummingbird flowers were abundant, hummingbird feeder visits dropped, and vice versa (Inouye 1991). And one fall when I filmed Ruby-throats and Buff-bellied hummingbirds near Corpus Christi, Texas, I noted these birds fed more from turk's cap than at feeders. Apparently hummingbirds prefer genuine nectar, when it is available, over imitation nectar.

A century ago, millions of hummingbirds were killed and skinned by our forebears. The glittering hummingbird skins were used to adorn European ladies' hats and clothing. Three thousand hummingbird skins of one species made up a single shipment from a port in Brazil in the late 1800s. In 1888, twelve thousand hummingbird skins moved through markets during one month in London. In one year alone the London markets sold four hundred thousand "bird skins." Considering the demand for hummingbird skins at that time, it is reasonable to assume a large number of those four hundred thousand bird skins came from hummingbirds.

Today, feathered skins displayed in some European museums are from hummingbirds collected in the nineteenth century. Many of these museum specimens are species that have not been rediscovered living in the wild. The brightest and best-colored hummingbirds were probably the most sought after and therefore the first to go. Maybe there was a time when more than one species of hummer flew with the Ruby-throated, brightening eastern flowerscapes. When a flower petal moves on a calm sunny day, could the petal have moved because of air stirred by the wings of a visiting hummingbird spirit?

Segments of society talk about "having it all." If natural gifts are "all," this miniature, condensed bundle of iridescent energy surely already has it. Hummingbirds have the gift of unmatched flying skills; the homing instinct of a carrier pigeon; the stamina of birds thousands of times their size; and engaging personalities. The little rascals are also ingenious, curious, perky, sometimes comical, always bright eyed, confident, and irrepressible. To top it off, they have colors pure as a rainbow. The bird may have a song too, possibly a song of angel-voiced music beyond the range of human hearing.

With nearly every hummingbird breed in the U.S. and Canada

thriving, and with new and old species expanding northward and east-ward from Mexico, we have an opportunity to meet and encourage these joyful, optimistic, cheerful, intelligent little birds.

It appears part of the hummingbird's future is in our hands. This time we seem to be doing it right.

Guide to
North American
Hummingbirds

Of the twenty-three hummingbirds reported in the United States and Canada, sixteen are known to build nests and breed there. Five of these sixteen are rare or infrequent U. S.-Canadian breeders. The following photographs of the sixteen breeding species were selected according to their usefulness for species identification.

Dr. William H. Baltosser, University of Arkansas at Little Rock, pioneered a method of identifying difficult species of hummingbirds from tail feather patterns (Baltosser 1987). Bill discovered a way to "read" tail feather shapes and designs like we use fingerprints for identity. Before Bill's findings were published, identifying adult female and male and female juvenile hummingbirds of some species was a formidable job.

I am fortunate to have met Bill at the beginning of my hummingbird photography. Without Bill's expertise, and his examination of my photographs, it would have been virtually impossible to bring forth an accurate collection of male and female photos of the species pictured in this section. Also, to the warm-hearted people who let me film hummingbirds in their backyards across Mexico, the United States, and Canada, "Thanks." And, in Albuquerque, Bruce Matthews brought to my attention the newly introduced freeze focus camera. This reduced my workload and shortened the time span necessary to acquire the photographs.

When using the photos for identification, note that occasionally an individual may have patches of pollen about its head, breast, or beak. Pollen patches are usually golden.

In addition to photographs, biographical sketches in this section describe each species. A distribution map depicts each bird's range. The maps, however, are less accurate and less up-to-date than the listing of "Where found" for each individual bird.

89

Where a state is listed as having a particular hummingbird, refer to the "State and Province Species List" (p. 183) for spring and fall migratory dates, plus flowers hummingbirds feed from in specific locations.

ALLEN'S HUMMINGBIRD

Selasphorus sasin

Origin of common name: Named after Charles A. Allen,
who discovered the bird.

Male Allen's

Where found: Alabama, Arizona (south), coastal California and Channel Islands, Florida, Louisiana, Massachusetts (Nantucket Island, August 1988), Mississippi, Missouri, Nevada, New Jersey, Oregon, Texas, British Columbia (Vancouver Island)

Winters: California and Mexico, including Baja

Specifications: One side of mature migrating male (*sasin*) wing averages 37.8 mm; mature migrating female 41.6 mm. Male (*sasin*) weights average 3.13 g; females 3.24 g. Notice that females are larger than males. Resident birds are slightly larger than the migrating subspecies; the difference is not detectable by eye. Some Allen's migrate between Baja and coastal Califor-

Female Allen's

nia. Others are California residents, concentrated on Santa Catalina, San Clemente, and other Channel Islands, with a few specimens on California's mainland, especially along the Palos Verdes Peninsula.

The Allen's is difficult to separate from Rufous hummingbirds when identifying in the field, especially females and immatures. Mature male Allen's and Rufous have bright Rufous sides. However, the Allen's has a metallic bronze-green head and back, whereas male Rufous hummingbirds have bright orange backs. Also, adult male Allen's sometimes have a small white area on the underside of its wing near the wing root. Adult male Rufous hummers don't have this marking. Female and immature Allen's and Rufous are so similar, an expert is often needed for accurate identification.

Migrant Allen's begin moving northward from wintering grounds in the

Valley of Mexico and Morelos (Phillips 1975) into southern California beginning in January. Around April, they are often seen in Ramsey Canyon, Arizona. Sometimes migrant Allen's come in large numbers to Ramsey, and sometimes singly or in pairs. Often they are back in Ramsey in late August. Although the Allen's is a fairly common visitor to the Mile Hi, they remain only a week or two, apparently passing through on their way to or from some destination unknown. (Allen's, Anna's, and Costa's are considered to be the only species that winter in the United States.)

To date, only four banded Allen's have been recovered away from their banding site. The longest distance between banding and recovery has been 504 miles (806 km) from California to Arizona. A flight of 482 miles (771 km) from San Francisco to San Diego, California, was recorded. Two other birds were banded and recovered on Point Reyes, California after flights of approximately 15 miles.

During courtship, the speed of this hummingbird during the fastest part of its dive has been calculated at between 52 and 72 miles per hour (Pearson 1960). Mating has been described as occuring in mid-air (Orr 1939).

On the west coast, Allen's hummingbirds are known to nest as far north as Bend, Oregon. These birds seem to prefer damp ravines and canyons, especially in a fog belt. Allen's nests range from inches above the ground in low brush (blackberry is common) to fifty feet high in trees. Nesting occurs from late January to late March. I have noted nesting activity by resident Allen's on the Palos Verdes peninsula near Los Angeles early in February. In San Francisco, migrant Allen's have been observed nesting in early May. Two eggs in that nest hatched after fifteen day's incubation. The birds fledged twenty-two and twenty-five days later (Orr 1939). Two nestings per season are common.

Since male Allen's and Rufous look so alike, whether the Allen's is more common to the eastern United States than presently thought remains to be seen (Andrews & Baltosser 1989). Until we have more proof, one can't automatically assume that all hummingbirds with rusty plumage east of the Mississippi River are Rufous hummingbirds, although Rufous is still more likely than Allen's (Conway & Drennan 1979).

California biologists estimate that the drought of the 1980s and 1990s reduced Allen's populations in the state by as much as 90 percent. Feeders available to the birds during this period probably saved many hummingbird lives.

Allen's hummingbirds rank fifteenth in size among the sixteen that breed in the United States and Canada.

Allen's

Allen's hummingbird breeding and wintering range.

Habitation areas
New sightings

ANNA'S HUMMINGBIRD

Calypte anna
Origin of common name: After Princess Anna Massena,
wife of François V. Massena, the Duke of Rivoli,
for whom Rivoli's hummingbird was named.

Male Anna's

<u>Where found</u>: Alabama, Alaska (SE), Arizona (south), Arkansas, California, Colorado, Idaho, Louisiana, Montana, Nevada (south), New Mexico, Oregon, Texas (except north), Utah, Washington, Wisconsin, British Columbia (Vancouver Island resident).

<u>Winters</u>: United States, Canada, and Mexico

<u>Specifications</u>: One side of a male's wing averages 49.7 mm; females 49.6 mm. Male weights average 4.31 g; females 4.07 g.

The Anna's is the most common hummingbird in southern California,

96

Female Anna's

and is more easily seen there than anywhere else. Sightings of this bird are increasing in Arizona; recently it has become the most common humming-bird found at Ramsey Canyon, Madera Canyon, and nearby Green Valley, Arizona, in late summer and early fall.

Anna's, Allen's, and Costa's are the only hummingbirds that are year-round residents of the United States or Canada. Anna's normally winter in southern Arizona and southern California. A few also live year-round on Vancouver Island, British Columbia.

Male Anna's not only have colorful gorgets, they also have iridescent crowns to match. This species is also only one of three U.S.-Canadian hummingbirds that supposedly sings, but its voice is little more than a first-class squeak, generally uttered from a perch. (Costa's and Berylline are also alleged to sing.)

Although most numerous during the winter months in southern California, Anna's are plentiful there in all seasons. The most favorable time for attracting Anna's with backyard feeders is during mid-summer's dry season, when flowers have become less plentiful. Females have a reputation for being more aggressive than males around feeders.

Generally, the Anna's prefer elevations below 5,000 feet. In desert heat, however, they migrate for the summer up into mountains where it is cooler. Anna's are commonly found on Tucson's Mount Lemmon during hot months.

Molting occurs in November and December in southern Arizona. Courtship has been observed as early as November 20 (Woods 1931). Breeding follows, beginning as early as the last days of December, making it one of the earliest breeders of U.S. birds. Early breeding is possible because of winter-blooming plants common to the southwest. Apparently the birds take advantage of these early flowers ahead of migrating hummingbirds that move northward from Mexico. In Tucson, nesting Anna's are common by mid-January.

The Anna's is the largest hummingbird found on the west coast. It is also a regular visitor to sapsucker wells.

In courtship the male lofts upward until almost out of sight. From aloft, its dive is nearly vertical at high speed and ends in a zoom past the beak of his perched female, where he chirps a chirp resembling the warning bark of the California ground squirrel. Past the female he swings up and back to a point directly above her. J.H. Bowles writing in the July 1910 *Condor* claims incubation time for Anna's eggs is seventeen days.

Many Anna's leave Arizona and southern California in the spring and fan out into states northward and eastward. A juvenile male was photographed by the author in December 1989 at Amarillo, Texas. In late August the birds retreat toward southern Arizona and California.

To date, a total of three Anna's that were banded have been recovered away from their banding site. The longest flight was 414 miles (662 km) by a young male banded in Ramsey Canyon, Arizona, October of 1990, and recovered April 1991 near Apple Valley, California.

In September of 1979, an adult male was banded near Tucson, Arizona, and recovered 5 miles away in September 1980.

Another adult male was banded at Sonoita, Arizona, in September 1989 and recovered 16 miles away, near Canelo, Arizona, in April of 1991.

Anna's rank eighth in size among the sixteen U.S./Canadian breeding hummingbirds.

Anna's

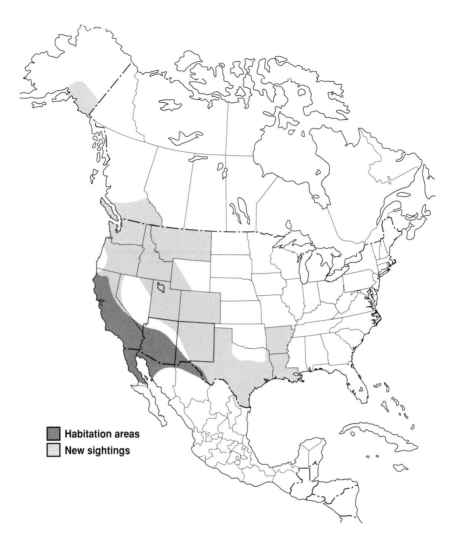

Anna's hummingbird breeding and wintering range.

BERYLLINE HUMMINGBIRD
Amazilia beryllina

Male Berylline

<u>Where found</u>: Extreme southeast Arizona, where it breeds rarely in the Chiricahua Mountains

<u>Winters</u>: Mountains of Mexico, from Alamos south

<u>Specifications</u>: One side of male wing averages 55.5 mm; females average 53.9 mm. Weights of males average 4.87 g; females 4.37 g. Notice that females are smaller than males.

    The Berylline is a rare hummingbird in the U.S. and Canada, and a rare breeder there. It is primarily a tropical hummingbird of Mexico's mountains. Most tropical hummingbirds that drift into the southern limits of the United States have brighter colors than more common North American hummers. Emerald green is the Berylline's prime coloration with touches of rust and

Berylline

Female Berylline

a hint of purple on its rump and on some wing and tail feathers. The bird's gorget is a brighter green than its sides and back.

In Arizona's Ramsey Canyon, records indicate a pair of Berylline hummers nested there in July 1976. A pair has also nested near Willcox. Then, on June 21, 1991, in Ramsey Canyon, a Berylline built the fourth known nest in the United States. Beryllines have also been sighted in Madera Canyon; around Comfort Springs; near the Natural Bridge Trailhead parking area in the Chiricahua National Monument; and near Portal in Cave Creek Canyon; Silver Creek Spring; and Spofford's sanctuary, all in Arizona.

I have seen only one Berylline nest. Below that nest, suspended on spider webbing, were a few blades of grass, twisting in the wind like silent wind chimes.

To date, only one banded Berylline hummingbird has been recaptured away from its banding site. In July of 1987, a Berylline was banded in Ramsey Canyon, Arizona. In September that same year the bird was recaptured in Madera Canyon, forty miles distant.

This species is one of the three U.S.-Canadian hummingbirds that is said to sing, although its voice is little more than a squeak. (Costa's and Anna's are also alleged to sing.)

Beryllines are generalist foragers (Des Grange 1979).

This hummingbird ranks fourth in size among the sixteen breeding species found in Canada and the U.S.

Berylline

■ **Habitation areas**

Berylline hummingbird breeding and wintering range.

103

BLACK-CHINNED HUMMINGBIRD
Archilochus alexandri

Male Black-chinned

Where found: Alabama, Arizona, Arkansas, California, Colorado (south and west), Florida, Georgia, Idaho, Kansas, Louisiana, Mississippi, Montana, Nevada, New Mexico, North Carolina, Oklahoma, Oregon, Texas, Utah, Washington, Wyoming (NW), British Columbia, Nova Scotia, Ontario, Saskatchewan

Winters: Mexico, including Baja

Specifications: One side of a male's wing averages 42.7 mm; females 47 mm. Male weights average 3.09 g; females 3.42 g. Notice that females are larger than males.

The Black-chinned is the third most widely distributed hummingbird in

Black-chinned

Female Black-chinned
(Male and female juveniles are similar.)

the United States and Canada after Rufous and Ruby-throated. It is also the least colorful of hummingbirds that breed in the United States.

To date, a total of five banded Black-chinned hummingbirds have been recovered. In 1991, one became the first hummingbird that was documented both in the United States and on its wintering grounds in Mexico. This male was banded by Steve Russell at Sonoita, Arizona, in July 1988 and recovered in April 1991 approximately 32 miles north-northeast of Manzanillo, Mexico. This flight is the fifth longest documented hummingbird distance: 930 miles (1488 km). (A Rufous hummingbird currently holds higher distance records.) Other records include a bird banded near San Jose, California in August 1989 and found dead 233 miles (373 km) away at Redding, California. Another Black-chinned was banded at Sapillo Creek, New Mexico, May 13, 1991, and recaptured May 28, 1993, 67 miles (107 km) away at Clifton, Arizona.

In September of 1988, a young female was banded in Ramsey Canyon, Arizona, and recovered 45 miles away, at Sonoita, Arizona, in July 1989.

In April of 1991, an adult male was banded at Sonoita and recaptured two months later, 16 miles away, near Canelo, Arizona.

The oldest documented age of a Black-chinned is 4 years 9 months (North American Bird Bander, July/September 1988).

Black-chinned eggs require fourteen days' incubation in New Mexico (author's observations in 1990 and 1991; Adele Thompson May 1994, plus Ryan Johnson May–June 1994). In Albuquerque, Ryan Johnson discovered a nest under construction May 16, 1994. He noted the first egg at 3:00 p.m. May 19. (Other nests in the area were known ten days earlier). He discovered the second egg two days later at noon May 21. He observed a second female harass the nest-building female for three days after the mother-to-be had laid her first egg.

Incubation didn't begin until noon May 22, 24 hours after the second egg had been laid. In previous years I noted that incubation began as much as a day after both eggs were in the nest. It seems reasonable to assume that the reason the hen waits a day before beginning incubation is to allow both eggs to stabilize at the same temperature. Such a procedure should bring both eggs to term at about the same time. Her strategy may be to eliminate a staggered hatch, and subsequent staggered fledge times. That would cut a day or two off the energy she would be required to expend on providing food for a holdover "staggered" nestling. The eggs in the nest Johnson observed did hatch the same day, eight and a half hours apart. They also fledged on the same day.

In 1990, 1991, and 1994 I observed a fledge time of 23 days. Ryan Johnson also had a fledge time of 23 days in May–June 1994. (In 1970 in Arizona, an incubation period of 16 days and a fledge time of 22 days was noted [Demaree 1970].)

On two occasions I have observed a female Black-chinned building a second nest before chicks in her first nest fledged. Nest-building time in this instance was three days. She seemed to handle her triple-duty chores of feeding herself, feeding her young, and building a new nest (in the same fruitless mulberry tree) for her second set of eggs. And in southern California a female Black-chinned completed three nesting sequences in one season (Cogswell 1949). Males tend to vacate a feeder used by a nesting female, presumably to assure ample food for females and young.

Black-chins rank eleventh in size among sixteen hummingbirds that breed in the U.S. and Canada.

Black-chinned

Black-chinned breeding and wintering range.

Habitation areas
New sightings

BLUE-THROATED HUMMINGBIRD
Lampornis clemencia (Lesson)

Male Blue-throated
Photograph by Ed Brown

<u>Where found</u>: Arizona (SE), California (south), Colorado, New Mexico (SW), Texas (west), Utah

<u>Winters</u>: Mexico

<u>Specifications</u>: One side of a male's wing averages 76.7 mm; females 69.7 mm. Male weights average 8.4 g; females 6.8 g.

Although Blue-throated hummingbirds are considered a Mexican hummingbird, a number spend the summer and breed in southeast Arizona and southwest New Mexico. In the highlands of the Chisos Mountains of Big Bend National Park, Texas, this hummingbird is the most common hummer in cypress-pine-oak areas from June through mid-August. Before flowering occurs, males feed only on insects, picking them from vegetation as well as

Blue-throated

Female Blue-throated

catching them on the fly, especially above creekbeds. After flowering, insects continue to be central in this hummingbird's diet throughout summer (Kuban 1980). Blue-throateds tend to establish territories near a stream. Blue-throated hummers are also occasionally reported as far north as Colorado and Utah. It is the largest hummingbird in the United States, followed in size by the Magnificent (Rivoli's).

Flight of the Blue-throated is jerky compared with most hummingbirds. This bird rapidly flaps, "coasts," rapidly flaps, "coasts," etc. It quickly displays tail feathers with conspiciously white-spotted outer tips. Blue-throated and male White-eared are the only North American hummingbirds with white-tipped tail feathers.

Blue-throateds occasionally overwinter in southern Arizona, but it is more common for them to winter in Mexico and return to the United States in February. When the Blue-throated does winter in Arizona, it feeds on insects found under the eaves of suburban homes and cottages, as well as taking insects and nectar from old sapsucker wells.

Blue-throated males tend to assemble in mating arenas called leks, where they "sing" and compete in courtship rituals to attract females. Birds that assemble in mating arenas are considered to be more primitive and less developed than other hummingbirds.

Females are very selective about nesting sites. The nest must be sheltered from both sun and rain, within easy distance of nectar producing flowers, and near a stream. Blue-throated have been located under bridges, even under the eaves of streamside houses. (Blue-throateds will rarely nest in a streamside tree.) Once a site is selected, the female uses that nest year after year, sometimes rebuilding atop old nests. After repeated rebuilding, these nests are nearly a foot high. Carroll Peabody recorded a Blue-throated nest that was used twelve consecutive years in Ramsey Canyon, Arizona. Blue-throateds often raise two broods per season.

During one nesting season in Ramsey Canyon, Carroll watched a male Blue-throated perch in a tree that gave him surveillance over the nests of three females. When one of the females would leave her nest to feed at a feeder, this male would speed from his perch and herd her back to her nest. One day, one of the females left her nest, and rather than go toward a feeder she hummed off into the woods. The male followed, attempting to herd her back. As soon as the two were out of sight, the other two females left their nests, flew straight to the feeder, and fed. After three days of being decoyed into the woods by one or the other of the females, the male abandoned his female-watching perch.

The oldest known Blue-throated is a bird that was banded in Arizona and shifted forty miles between Ramsey and Madera canyons. This bird was documented at six years old. Other banding records include two males that were banded at Ramesy Canyon, Arizona, and recaptured twenty-six hours later in Madera Canyon.

Since larger hummingbirds expend more energy in hover than smaller species, perches on feeders may be important in attracting Blue-throats.

Blue-throated

Habitation areas
New sightings

Blue-throated breeding and wintering range.

BROAD-BILLED HUMMINGBIRD
Cynanthus latirostris (Swainson)

Male Broad-billed

<u>Where found</u>: Arizona (south), California, Louisiana, Nevada, New Mexico (far SW), Texas (west and south), Utah, Ontario

<u>Winters</u>: Mexico (common in Guadalajara).

<u>Specifications</u>: One side of a male's wing averages 54.8 mm; females 53.2 mm (Moore 1939b). Male weights average 3.72 g; females 3.4 g (Johnsgard 1983).
    Broad-bills are the second most common hummingbird (behind Black-chins) in Madera Canyon, forty miles south of Tucson, Arizona. There are a few in Ramsey Canyon. Dr. David Ferry's banding records through 1991 show 808 Broad-billed birds in Madera, compared with 10 in Ramsey Canyon. (The same period shows 1,290 Black-chinned in Madera.) Madera

Broad-billed

Female Broad-billed

Canyon is probably the easiest place in the United States to see this colorful bird.

In late March and early April, Broad-bills arrive in Madera, in prime color. This hummingbird stays in Arizona until late August. In eastern Arizona the bird is rare, but is occasionally seen at Portal. It is also occasionally in southwest New Mexico, especially in or near Guadalupe Canyon.

The Broad-billed is larger than the average hummingbird. It is also noisy, chattering constantly while in flight. Bill Baltosser describes this hummer's chattering as sounding like two quarter-inch steel balls rattling in one's hand, crap shooter style. (Violet-crowns make a similar sound, but only as an alarm call.) It is my observation that where Broad-bills occur with Costa's (rare) the noisy Broad-bills dominate. Since Costa's are much smaller than

Broad-bills, and therefore capable of flying circles around them, it seems likely that Costa's are buffaloed by the Broad-bill's chattering. And it seems probable that Broad-bills, since they are less nimble than smaller hummers, have developed chattering as a countermeasure to their maneuverability handicap.

Dr. Ferry suspects red coloring in the bird's bill intensifies with age.

Broad-bills commonly breed in Madera Canyon, Arizona.

To date, not a single banded Broad-billed has been recovered away from its banding site.

Broad-billed hummingbirds rank sixth in size among hummers breeding in the United States or Canada.

Broad-billed

Habitation areas
New sightings

Broad-billed breeding and wintering range.

BROAD-TAILED HUMMINGBIRD
Selasphorus platycercus (Swainson)

Male Broad-tailed
(Note "whistle slot" in wing tip.)

<u>Where found</u>: Arizona, California, Colorado, Florida, Georgia, Idaho, Kansas, Louisiana, Montana, Nebraska, Nevada, New Mexico, Oregon (east), South Dakota, Texas (except east), Utah, Wyoming

<u>Winters</u>: Mexico

<u>Specifications</u>: One side of a male's wing averages 48.4 mm; females 49.9 mm. Male weights average 3.16 g; females 3.6 g. Notice that females are larger than males.

   The mature male Broad-tailed is the only hummingbird that "hums" in normal, cross-country flight. "Staccato whistle" might be a better description than "hum." The bird's wing sound resembles that of a cricket singing a continuous tone, or the sound of a police or referee's whistle blown without

Broad-tailed

Female Broad-tailed

pause. The "whistling" is produced by a slot formed by tapered tips on the ninth and tenth primary wing feathers (see male's photo).

Speculation as to how the bird made its sound ended when Sarah J. Miller and David W. Inouye of the University of Maryland cemented the tips of the ninth and tenth primaries on a mature male Broad-Tail's wing feathers and created a silent flyer. In 1983 Miller and Inouye published their findings of a study of the Broad-tail's wing whistle in *Animal Behavior*. Their conclusion was that the bird's whistle is a form of territory claim, and is audible to the human ear just beyond the length of a football field, one hundred yards. The sound is pitched near F sharp, variable with altitude, temperature, the amount of wear on wing tip feathers that produce the sound, and the level of aggression mobilized by the bird against an intruder.

Bill Calder, at the University of Arizona, points out that by midwinter the male's feathers have worn so much, it has almost worn out its whistle. When it molts into new feathers, its whistle comes back up to speed, in time for spring mating season. There are indications that the sound's feedback stirs the birds' mating instincts.

Calder also discovered that when defending a territory, male Broad-tails (and probably other species as well) feed lightly during the day, taking on only 1–2 percent of their body weight through the day. Apparently this feeding behavior is in order for the birds to keep themselves light, and therefore more maneuverable against intruders. At dusk, when territory defense flights are shut down, Calder discovered the males gorge from 32–40 percent of their body weight.

The Broad-tailed is a western mountain hummingbird, breeding in the mountain states from the Mexican border nearly to the Canadian border. Summer blooming mountain wildflowers depend upon the Broad-tailed, as well as other hummingbirds, for pollination. These flowers include salvia, columbine, and Indian paintbrush. This hummingbird, along with the Ruby-throated, Rufous, and Calliope, is one of the northernmost breeders among U.S. and Canadian hummingbirds.

To date a total of five banded Broad-taileds have been recovered away from their banding sites. The longest recorded flight is that of a female banded August 17, 1991 at Sapillo Creek, New Mexico and recaptured July 11, 1992, 410 miles away (656 km) at Hotchkiss, Colorado. All other re-coveries were of flights made within Colorado, none beyond 44 miles of where the birds were banded.

A female holds the North American hummingbird age record—twelve years old. This Broad-tailed was banded and recovered at the same location, the Rocky Mountain Biological Laboratory near Gothic, Colorado.

Broad-tails rank ninth in size among the sixteen breeding species.

Broad-tailed

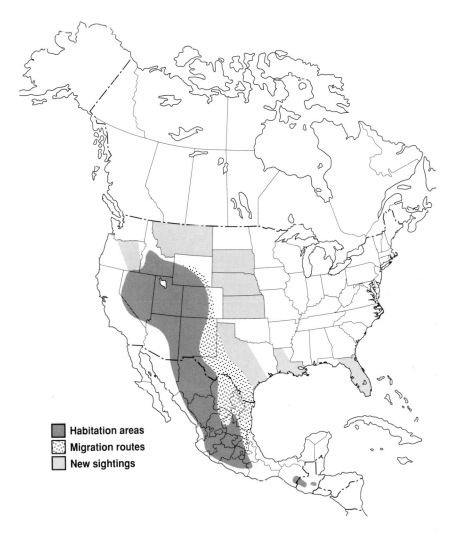

Habitation areas
Migration routes
New sightings

Broad-tailed hummingbird breeding and wintering range. Stippling depicts probable migration routes.

BUFF-BELLIED HUMMINGBIRD
(Fawn-breasted)
Trochilus yucatanensis (Cabot)

Buff-bellied
(Male and female are almost identical.) Photo courtesy of Robert Sutton.

<u>Where found</u>: Alabama, Arkansas, Florida, Georgia, Louisiana, Mississippi, Texas

<u>Winters</u>: Eastern Mexico, especially coastal states

<u>Specifications</u>: One side of a male's wing averages 53.8 mm; females 52.2 mm. Male weights average 4.05 g; females 3.67 g.

This bird is a minor U.S. breeding species. As hummingbirds go, the Buff-bellied is large, bigger than the Anna's but smaller than the Broad-billed. Buff-bellied nests are built in low bushes generally not over five feet above the ground. The bird nests in the Brownsville and Corpus Christi areas of

Buff-bellied hummingbird breeding and wintering range.

Texas. When foraging, the birds make a sound similar to that of a foraging Cardinal.

Loss of eastern and northeastern Mexico habitat to agriculture seems to be forcing the Buff-bellied more and more into the United States.

From an attempt to photograph a pair of Buff-bellieds in the Corpus Christi area I discovered this bird has a good memory. They had been filmed two months before by a photographer who used five flashes that were described as looking "like an atom bomb explosion." Apparently as a result of their earlier experience, the birds totally avoided the area where I set up my photo equipment. I abandoned the photo attempt after two days. (The photographer was kind enough to share his photos with me for publication in this work.)*

A few Buff-bellied overwinter at feeders along the south Texas coast, and once in a while a stray winters at a feeder in Louisiana.

To date, not a single banded Buff-bellied has been recovered away from its banding site.

The Buff-bellied ranks seventh in size among sixteen breeding species found in the U.S. and Canada.

*One year later, a Buff-bellied at the exact location near Corpus Christi totally avoided the vicinity where I again set up my photo equipment. Assuming the bird was the same, I again abandoned photography. Apparently the Buff-bellied has a long, possibly lifetime, memory of its experience with five powerful flash units.

CALLIOPE
Stellula calliope

Male Calliope

Where found: Arizona, California (including Santa Catalina Island), Colorado, Florida, Idaho, Kansas, Louisiana, Mississippi, Montana, Nebraska, Nevada, New Mexico, Oklahoma, Oregon (east and west), South Dakota, Texas (west, central, and panhandle), Utah, Washington, Wyoming, Alberta, British Columbia (including Vancouver Island), Saskatchewan

Winters: West-central Mexico

Specifications: One side of a male's wing averages 38.7 mm; females 42.8 mm. Male weights average 2.5 g; females 2.83 g. Notice that females are larger than males.

The male Calliope is the fourth smallest (wingspan) hummingbird found in the United States and Canada. Ruby-throated, Allen's, and Lucifer are smaller (Johnsgard 1983).

Calliope

Immature Male Calliope
(Almost identical to adult female.)

The most obvious identification features of the Calliope are that it is very small and has a stubby tail. When perched, this hummingbird's wing tips are even with its tail feathers or extend beyond them. Another identifier is that when feeding, the Calliope doesn't pump its tail the way many other hummingbirds do, especially the Black-chinned.

This bird perches low to the ground, and generally nests low. At the Arizona-Sonora Desert Museum, in Tucson, a feeder, specially placed for their captive Calliope, is about a foot off the ground. Down at that level the little bird pursues insects, suggesting this tiny bird's niche is within the first four or five feet above ground level. This is a clue to recognizing the bird. In the wild, it flies low and stays low, rarely getting above five feet. Attracting this hummingbird with a feeder would best be done with one located no higher than four feet.

Calliopes arrive at the Mile Hi in Arizona in April during northward migration. Although the species may stay a couple of weeks, generally it moves on toward breeding grounds in northwestern mountain states.

The Calliope is a high mountain bird, and has been seen as high as 11,000 feet. Nests are almost always built over creeks, or over roads and trails next to streams and lakes. Nests are most common in coniferous trees, built near the end of the lowermost living limb. The nests are either saddled on the main stem or on the junction of a horizontal fork. Few nests are more than two hundred yards from a stream or other body of water. The birds almost always repair an old nest, or build a new nest atop an old one from year to year. Individual females build nests in such a way that they bear that bird's "signature" and look like no other (Weydemeyer 1927). Even though the Calliope has a reputation of living low in mountain pines, it has been found (rarely) nesting as high as 70 feet.

Calliope migration is circular, and tends to follow the wind field associated with an average-sized Great Basin High pressure center. Some are showing up in the east, suggesting a few may ride the winds of a super Great Basin High, as the Rufous does. A couple of Calliope have been banded by Bob Sargent in mid-winter in southeastern states.

To date, three banded Calliopes have been recovered away from their banding site. In June 1987, an adult female was banded in Libby, Montana. Two years later, in July 1989, this hummer was recovered 773 miles (1,237 km) away, in Gothic, Colorado. The second was banded in the San Bernardino Mountains, California, July 1990 and recovered 434 miles (694 km) in September 1990 at Sonoita, Arizona. A shorter flight was documented by a young bird banded near Big Bear City, California, in July 1990 and recovered 410 miles (656 km) away two months later near Canelo, Arizona.

Another female Calliope was banded in Condon, Montana in June 1982 and recovered a second time six years later, July 1988, in Condon. In 1991, Calder and Jones encountered two other Calliopes in Montana that were six years old (personal communication with Elly Jones 1992).

Calliopes, along with Ruby-throated, Rufous, and Broad-tailed, are the northernmost U.S. and Canadian breeders.

The Calliope ranks thirteenth in size among the sixteen species.

Calliope

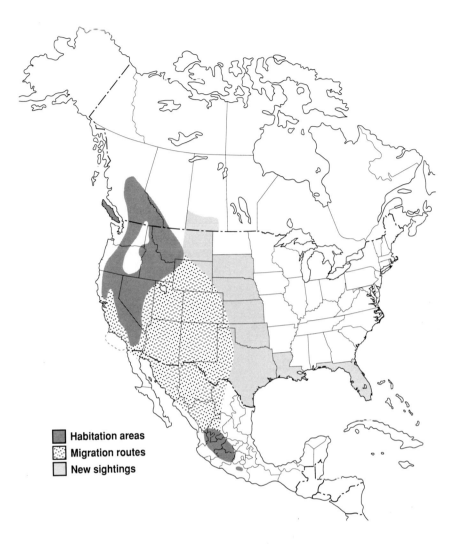

Calliope hummingbird breeding and wintering range.

Habitation areas
Migration routes
New sightings

COSTA'S HUMMINGBIRD
Calypte costae
Origin of common name: Named after French nobleman
M. le Margins Costa de Beauregard

Male Costa's

<u>Where found</u>: Alaska (once), Arizona, California (including Santa Catalina Island), Nevada, New Mexico, Oregon (west), rarely in west and central Texas, Utah (SW), rare in British Columbia (including Vancouver Island)

<u>Winters</u>: SE California (and coastal islands), SW Arizona, NW Sonora, Baja (and coastal islands)

<u>Specifications</u>: One side of a male's wing averages 44.4 mm; females 44.7 mm. Male weights average 3.05 g; females 3.22 g. Notice that females are larger than males.

Costa's don't migrate across much distance. In late January, they move

128

Female Costa's

from Baja and Mexico's northwest coast into the deserts of southern California and southwestern Arizona shortly after winter rains have awakened desert flowering. Along with some swallows, they are the first birds to arrive in spring, sometimes as early as late January. (Throughout winter, a few Costa's are seen at feeders in southern California and Arizona.)

Courtship begins soon after spring migration. Males diving for attention from females produce a sound resembling the shriek of a ricocheting bullet. The whine is prolonged and may be vocal, since a similar sound is produced by a perched bird (Wells 1978). As a result of sounds the males produce, this hummingbird is only one of three species found in North America credited with having a "song." (Anna's and Berylline are the others.) The distinctive sound of the Costa's is an aid in field identification. Mating follows the male's courtship flight.

Females generally choose nest sites in lower elevation desert areas, such as in Organ Pipe Cactus National Monument, Arizona, or Joshua Tree National Monument, California. Typically, Costa's nest a considerable distance from surface water, and several nests may be located in one area. Incubation is believed to average about sixteen days. Costa's sometimes nest in the Phoenix area as early as late January. Southern California has a nesting record as early as February 3 (Bakus 1962). Nest heights vary between 3 and 10 feet, but are more often at around 5 feet (Woods, 1927).

Around mid-May, when Arizona's temperatures climb into the hundreds and the desert becomes even drier, flowering diminishes and the birds "disappear." No banding records verify where they go. When I heard of this phenomenon, I suspected they flew up into the cooler elevations of Arizona's desert mountains (dry desert air cools 5.5° F per 1,000 feet of altitude), in the way Black-chins, Anna's, Broad-tails, and Magnificents hum up into the cool of Tucson's Mount Lemmon. (Banding records don't prove Costa's populate Mount Lemmon.) Baltosser believes the birds scatter more to the west and northwest, or even back into Mexico. His study of the Costa's shows the birds' presence increases in the mountains of Southern California, southern Nevada, northwestern Arizona, and extreme southwestern Utah, between March 16 and June 30 (Baltosser 1989). This is a time when mountain flowers would blossom from plants irrigated by winter's melting snow. At Lake Havasu State Park, Arizona wildlife officials said large numbers of Costa's pass there in May (personal communication). This suggests that Costa's may migrate in early summer up the Colorado River, into the cooler mountains around Kingman, Arizona, and the mountains near Palm Springs, California, southern Nevada, and extreme southwestern Utah. In October, the birds reappear in Arizona, foraging among new desert flowers brought forth by summer monsoon rains.

Since Costa's mate again in April and May, after their first brood fledges, and before they become scarce in the face of rising summer heat, they may raise a second brood in the mountains. From hatch to fledge is 22 days.

To date, not a single banded Costa's has been recovered away from its banding site.

Of the sixteen breeding species in Canada and North America, the Costa's ranks tenth in size.

Costa's

Habitation areas
New sightings

Costa's hummingbird breeding and wintering range.

LUCIFER HUMMINGBIRD
Calothorax lucifer (Swainson)

Male Lucifer

<u>Where found</u>: Arizona (SE), New Mexico (SW), Texas (Big Bend area)

<u>Winters</u>: Central Mexico

<u>Specifications</u>: One side of a male's wing averages 37.6 mm; females 41.2 mm. Male weights average 2.75 g; females 3.08 g. Notice that females are larger than males.

Male Lucifer hummingbirds are the smallest in North America. The Calliope is fourth smallest (Johnsgard 1983). Male Lucifers, with magenta gorgets, light underparts, that unique downcurved beak, and small size are easy to identify. This is the only North American hummer with a beak that is downcurved (or decurved). Its unusual beak is made even more so by its long length.

Lucifer

Female Lucifer

Lucifer hummingbirds are known to migrate into the southwestern United States only. Between early March and mid-September, Lucifer hummers are fairly common in the Chisos mountains of the Texas Big Bend area, especially along Window Trail, in washes near Panther Junction, and in Blue Creek Canyon (personal communication with Peter Scott, 1992). In mid-July, ten Lucifers were observed along one-half mile of the South Rim (Chisos Mountains) at an elevation of about 7,500 feet. In mid-September, no Lucifers were seen in that same area, although there were many Rufous (Fox 1954).

Breeding in the Big Bend area is common between April and early August; Lucifers also commonly breed 30 miles east of Douglas, Arizona, and across the border at Arroyo Cajon Bonito, Mexico, near the New Mexico, Arizona, Mexico border (Russell 1978). In Arizona a nesting Lucifer was found in Guadalupe Canyon east of Douglas. In addition, several pairs breed yearly in the Peloncillo Mountains of extreme southwestern New Mexico. And nearly every year there is at least one male Lucifer in Ramsey Canyon, Arizona. A few others summer in Cave Creek, Arizona.

This hummingbird has a preference for flowering agaves.

The Lucifer is probably the least impacted by feeders of United States and Canadian hummers.

Lucifer's smaller size renders it more maneuverable, and therefore capable of holding its own when defending feeding grounds against larger tropical hummingbirds such as the Blue-throated, Magnificent, Violet-crowned, and Broad-billed.

To date, not a single banded Lucifer hummingbird has been recovered away from its banding site.

Lucifer

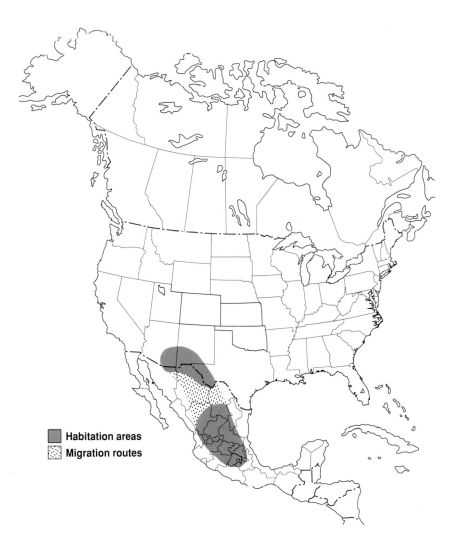

Habitation areas
Migration routes

Lucifer hummingbird breeding and wintering range.

MAGNIFICENT (RIVOLI) HUMMINGBIRD
(Eugenes fulgens)

Male Magnificent

<u>Where found</u>: Arizona (SE), Arkansas, Colorado (south), Georgia, Kansas, Nevada, New Mexico (SW), Texas (west), Utah, Wyoming

<u>Winters</u>: Mexico

<u>Specifications</u>: One side of a male's wing averages 73 mm; females 68.7 mm. Male weights average 7.7 g; females 6.4 g.

The Magnificent is the second largest hummingbird in the United States (Blue-throated is larger). Carroll Peabody recalls that when he had the Mile Hi, a dead plum tree was often loaded with as many as seventy-five to a hundred male Magnificent hummingbirds at one time . . . unusual for a bird considered to be a loner. Near dusk each day, these males would fly en masse, as if on signal, and swoop down on other hummingbirds feeding at

Magnificent (Rivoli)

Female Magnificent

forty or so feeders spaced along a heavy wire support. The Magnificents' mass flight drove all other hummingbirds away from the feeders. As soon as the other hummers were gone, the flock of male Magnificents took perches near and around the feeders. Immediately the area's population of young Magnificents would descend upon the vacated feeders and feast. This event was singular because it is rare for male hummingbirds to contribute to the welfare of their young. For a couple of weeks this invasion of the feeder area by male Magnificents took place, each time just before dark. The mass flights continued each evening until the young were about a month old, and able to fend for themselves. (East of Douglas, Arizona, Paul Noack, foreman at Slaughter Ranch, reports seeing this same event.)

Magnificent hummingbirds nest high in trees, often near the tops of oak, sycamore, or pine. They like mountain country as high as 8,000 feet.

For some reason, Magnificents often stand their ground against the feisty Rufous. On these occasions this hummingbird squeaks in a voice described by Dan Ostler of Mogollon, New Mexico, as the sound of "a 1950s space fantasy ray gun." Generally, the Rufous seem unimpressed and refuse to yield.

Madera and Ramsey Canyons in Arizona are places where Magnificents are easily seen.

In New Mexico, Magnificents are common at the silver- and gold-mining ghost town of Mogollon, elevation 5,995 feet, and near the Continental Divide. The author saw several of these hummingbirds, with other species, there in late May 1991. The Magnificent hummingbird nests in both Arizona and New Mexico.

On a ranch near the Continental Divide and I-40 in New Mexico, between Gallup and Grants, a Magnificent is sometimes seen at feeders. Since this is a large hummingbird, it expends more energy in hover than smaller hummers. Therefore, perches on feeders are important to Magnificents. To conserve energy, this hummingbird often glides on rigid wings.

To date, only two Magnificents have been banded and later recovered. An adult male was banded in Madera Canyon, Arizona, in May 1988 and recovered approximately 200 miles (320 km) away in May 1991 near Safford, Arizona. Another was banded April 4, 1993, Ramsey Canyon, Arizona, and recovered 167 miles (267 km) away August 19, Sapillo Creek, New Mexico.

Of the sixteen breeding species in Canada and North America, the Magnificent ranks second in size (Johnsgard 1983).

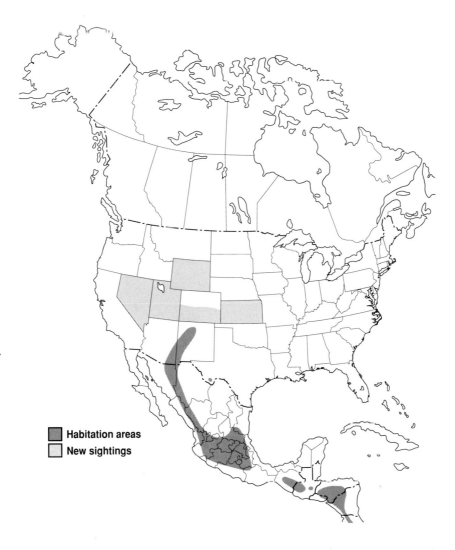

Magnificent (Rivoli) hummingbird breeding and wintering range.

RUBY-THROATED HUMMINGBIRD
Archilochus colubris

Male Ruby-throated

<u>Where found</u>: Alabama, Alaska, Arkansas, California (south), Connecticut, Delaware, District of Columbia, Florida, Georgia, Illinois, Indiana, Iowa, Kansas, Kentucky, Louisiana, Maine, Maryland, Massachusetts, Michigan, Minnesota, Mississippi, Missouri, Nebraska, New Hampshire, New Jersey, New Mexico, New York, North Carolina, North Dakota, Ohio, Oklahoma, Pennsylvania, Rhode Island, South Carolina, South Dakota, Tennessee, Texas, Vermont, Virginia, West Virginia, Wisconsin, Wyoming, Alberta, British Columbia (including Vancouver Island), Manitoba, New Brunswick, Newfoundland, Northwest Territories, Nova Scotia, Ontario, Prince Edward Island, Quebec, Saskatchewan, Cuba, the Bahama Islands, Hispaniola

<u>Winters</u>: Southern half of Mexico south to Panama; Cuba, the Bahamas, and Hispaniola (Haiti and the Dominican Republic)

140

Female Ruby-throated

<u>Specifications</u>: One side of a male's wing averages 38.5 mm; females 44.5 mm. Male weights average 3.03 g; females 3.34 g (5 plus g at migration). Notice that females are larger than males.

The Ruby-throated is the third smallest (wingspan) hummingbird that breeds in Canada and the U.S. (Johnsgard 1983). This bird was probably the first hummingbird seen by the colonists. In 1714, Englishman John Lawson, traveling the east coast, wrote in his diary, "The hummingbird is the miracle of all our winged animals. He is feathered as a bird, but gets his living as the bees. His nest is one of the greatest pieces of workmanship the whole tribe of winged animals can show."

The Ruby-throated is the second most widely distributed hummingbird in North America (Rufous is first, with the Ruby-throat's cousin the Black-chinned third. Ruby-throats and Black-chins may occasionally interbreed). It is interesting to note that these three birds are nearly the same size, which indicates their size may be close to optimal for North American humming-birds. The Ruby-throated has been observed in forty-one of the United States, plus eleven out of twelve Canadian provinces and territories and all states in the southern half of Mexico.

Ruby-throated hummingbirds are reputed (not proven) to fly 500 miles nonstop across the Gulf of Mexico on spring and fall migrations to and from their wintering grounds in the southern half of Mexico. When my mother told me of their feat she traced the little birds' supposed route on maps depicting ocean water in deep blue. At the time I was no more than five. It is understatement to say my child's mind was impressed. As an adult, thousands of hours of aircraft pilot experience have caused me to be skeptical. But, in the face of my skepticism, a field study indicates the little birds store enough fat relative to energy use to make the trip (Lasiewski 1962). Let's examine that mythical 500 mile nonstop trip.

Wind tunnel tests have established that a female Ruby-throat's cruising speed is 27 mph using 53 wingbeats per second ($\pm$ 3) (Greenewalt 1960b). At that rate, a female Ruby-throated would require 18 hours and 30 minutes to fly 500 miles in calm air. (A 10 mph tailwind would reduce the trip time to 13 hours and 30 minutes.)

Daylight hours in the gulf during spring and fall migration average about 12.5 hours. If a Ruby-throated took off 30 minutes before sunrise, which is the earliest I have seen hummingbirds fly, under calm air conditions that bird would be forced to fly in darkness and land 6 hours after sunset. On the other hand, a 10 mph tailwind with an en route time of 13 hours and 30 minutes is a marginal possibility . . . *if* the tailwind held.

I could be swayed toward embracing the 500-mile-nonstop idea by an eye expert's appraisal of the night vision of a Ruby-throated. At the moment, there is no evidence these birds fly at night. In fact, there is testimony to the contrary.

On the shore of Lake Erie, Ontario, Canada, a lighthouse stands 106 feet high on the tip of Long Point. Long Point is a major bird migration route. Further, it is the site of the first ever established bird observatory in North America (The Long Point Bird Observatory). The lighthouse on Long Point, unfortunately, is struck by night flying migrants. Stunned birds collected from the foot of the lighthouse are tabulated, rehabilitated, banded, and released; statistics of bodies of dead birds are also recorded. George Wallace, a biologist who directed the observatory's migration monitor program between 1986 and 1989, states: "In the 31 years the observatory has been in operation, we have never recorded either a stunned hummingbird, or a hummingbird body from the base of the lighthouse."

Ruby-throated

The record at the Long Point lighthouse supports the idea that either hummingbirds don't fly at night, or if they do, they don't hit objects that are struck by other night flyers. But, unlikely as it seems, suppose the little birds did fly at night, and suppose they did fly across the Gulf of Mexico, some of it in darkness. At the end of such a flight, it is reasonable to expect the bird would be hungry. Would the little bird then forage and feed in the dark? (Torpor until sunrise might solve that problem, if the bird could find a perch in the dark.)

I think it more likely Ruby-throated hummingbirds migrate to Mexico via two routes. One, a land route following the coasts of Mississippi, Alabama, Louisiana, and Texas. It is a fact that squadrons of Ruby-throats, probably from the North American midwest and western Canada, move down the Texas coast on their return to Mexico in September. A tribute to the mass of their numbers passing along the Coastal Bend is the Rockport-Fulton, Texas, annual "Hummer/Bird Celebration" held each fall. In that area the birds are seen sipping nectar from coastal flowers as they migrate south.

A second possible land-migration route, one that would serve eastern Ruby-throats, is south through eastern states and down the east coast to the tip of Florida. From Florida the birds could move toward Mexico by island hopping across the Florida Keys, sipping nectar from wild flowers (or feeders) as they go. There are clues hinting a Florida migration route may be operative.

Karen Strobel, who tabulates birds for the Audubon Society at Key Largo, reports that Ruby-throated (and a few Black-chinned) hummingbirds show up along the Florida Keys the first week in October. Farther down the Keys, Joseph Onderjko reports Ruby-throated hummingbirds (and Black-chins) appear in Key West in early October. Both Strobel and Onderjko observe that with advancing fall, hummingbird numbers decrease; however a few of the birds apparently spend the winter on Florida Key islands.

Support for the hypothesis that hummingbirds follow coastal routes and island hop comes again from Long Point in Ontario, Canada. Wallace notes that during the day, observers may see between 50 and 100 hummingbirds moving through the Long Point Bird Observatory's migration monitoring stations. (Total number would be higher, since some hummers pass unseen.) Although it is only 25 miles across Lake Erie to Pennsylvania's shore, the birds are rarely seen heading out, or reported by boaters, over open water. Rather, they seem to follow the shoreline southwest. One hundred and forty miles down the lakeshore, at Point Pelee National Park, the world class birding spot, Ruby-throated counts approximate the numbers passing Long Point. (Wallace states that peak fall migration time for Ruby-throats along Canada's Lake Erie shoreline is early September.)

A checklist of the birds of Cuba (Los Angeles Audubon Society 1982) lists Ruby-throated hummingbirds on that island. It seems probable that in the fall these birds fly from the Keys to Cuba, a distance of 95 miles from Key West. That the Cuban Emerald hummingbird has been verified in Florida suggests there is hummingbird traffic from Cuba to Florida.

As further evidence hummingbirds may island hop, both the Ruby-throated and Rufous have been verified in the Bahama Islands, and the Bahama Woodstar periodically shows up in Florida. Ruby-throats are also on bird checklists of Hispaniola, including Haiti and the Dominican Republic. And back in Canada, at Pelee Point, Ruby-throats are seen heading for islands only 7 miles (16 minutes) away, in the direction of Ohio's coast, 12 miles (27 minutes) distant. Other Ruby-throats may continue down Ontario's shore, taking the longer, overland route before turning south.

Continuing to assume migrating Ruby-throats hum to Cuba, the birds could fly there from Key West, Florida, in 3 hours and 30 minutes, at 27 mph. From Cuba's northern coast, hummers could proceed west along the Cuban coastline toward Mexico. For over 200 miles, those birds inclined to push toward Mexico could take nourishment from tropical flowers along the way. (I wouldn't be surprised to learn that many Ruby-throated hummingbirds skip Mexico in favor of wintering in Cuba, the Bahamas, and/or Hispaniola.)

At Cuba's western tip, the birds would face their longest overwater hop on a trip to Mexico, 122 miles across the Yucatan Channel, to Isla Mujeres, just off the coast of Yucatan. At 27 mph, that open-water crossing would require 4 hours and 30 minutes, nonstop. There are a couple of ways to verify or disprove either migration theory.

A test for the 500-mile, over-water, nonstop theory would be to place a healthy female Ruby-throated hummingbird that has achieved migration weight, 5.5 grams, in a wind tunnel with no place for the bird to perch. Turn the machine on for 18 hours and 30 minutes. At the end of that time, if the hummingbird was still humming, perches and nectar could be introduced, in darkness, and results observed. A wind tube test producing a negative outcome would probably draw attention from the Society for the Prevention of Cruelty to Animals. Such a wind tunnel test would suggest whether the non-stop-across-the-Gulf theory is viable. (Hummingbird bander Bob Sargent of Trussville, Alabama, reports that he sees Ruby-throats coming on shore in coastal Alabama "three to ten feet high and exhausted." These birds either flew non-stop from Mexico, or had been blown a few miles out to sea by stormy winds and were returning to land.)

To test whether these birds island hop from Florida to Mexico would require banding stations on Key West, Cuba, and the Yucatan peninsula. Just how many, if any, of the Ruby-throated (and Black-chinned) hummingbirds arrive in the Florida Keys during October and move along the theoretical island hopping route will remain unknown until banding reports become available.

The Gulf coast route could be verified by banding reports from Louisiana, Texas, and Mexico. Early September banding at Long Point in Ontario might prove valuable, since Ruby-throats passing there potentially arrive or depart at either the Rockport-Fulton, Texas, area or the Florida keys. (Beginning in 1992, an intensive fall hummingbird banding program will be initiated in the Rockport-Fulton hummingbird migration corridor. A first, the program is planned for three to five consecutive fall seasons.)

By whatever course the Ruby-throated chooses to fly to and from its winter home in Mexico, it remains a beautiful bird. My doubting the idea of a 500 mile nonstop flight across open water is not meant to be disrespectful. I'd be impressed by a 4-hour and 30-minute nonstop flight across the waters of the Yucatan Channel by such a tiny bird.

To date, only five banded Ruby-throats have been recovered away from their banding site. The longest documented distance was made by a young male, who took off from Grove, Oklahoma, in August 1992 and was found dead 719 miles (1,150 km) away, at Carlton, Minnesota in June 1993. The second longest journey is that of another young male, who took off from a point near Somerset, Pennsylvania, in September 1980. A year and ten months later the little fellow's body was found 618 miles (993 km) away, in Quebec, Canada.

In July of 1983, an adult female bird was banded south of Grove, Oklahoma. In September of 1985 this bird was found dead 497 miles (799 km) distant, in Kerrville, Texas. September 1991, another Ruby-throated was banded at York, South Carolina. Fourteen days later this bird was recaptured 162 miles (259 km) away, at Loganville, Georgia. In 1986, near Chester, South Carolina, a young female was banded. A year later, this hummer was found only 10 miles away, near Rock Hill, South Carolina.

Banding records have established the age of two Ruby-throated hummingbirds at nine years, last captured in 1986 and 1989. Two others, aged eight, were last captured in 1984.

At one time the Ruby-throated was thought to be the only hummingbird found east of the Mississippi River. Now we know at least ten other hummingbirds occur east of that river. They are: Allen's, Rufous, Calliope, Anna's, Buff-bellied, Black-chinned, Bahama Woodstar, Broad-tailed, Green violet-eared, and Cuban Emerald.

It is likely that Ruby-throated hummingbirds were the first to be artificially fed in the United States by humans. These birds also feed regularly at sapsucker wells.

As a general rule, Ruby-throateds are not backyard nesters. They seem to require an isolated environment for breeding. Egg incubation for this hummingbird is fourteen days, and they are known to raise two broods in a season (Prowse 1934, Nickell 1948). Fledge time is seventeen to eighteen days after hatch (Nickell 1948).

The Ruby-throated ranks fourteenth in size among sixteen humming-birds that breed in the U.S. and Canada.

Ruby-throated

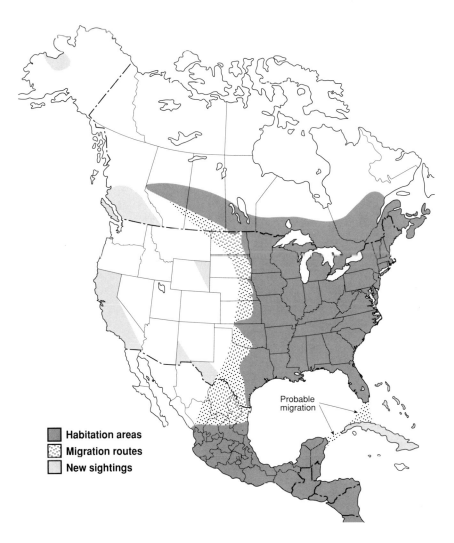

Habitation areas
Migration routes
New sightings

Probable migration

Ruby-throated hummingbird breeding and wintering range. Stippling depicts probable migration routes.

RUFOUS HUMMINGBIRD

Selasphorus rufus

Male Rufous

<u>Where found</u>: Alabama, Alaska, Arizona, Arkansas, California, Colorado, Connecticut, Delaware, District of Columbia, Florida, Georgia, Idaho, Illinois, Indiana, Iowa, Kansas, Kentucky, Louisiana, Maine, Maryland, Massachusetts, Michigan, Minnesota, Mississippi, Missouri, Montana, Nebraska, Nevada, New Hampshire, New Jersey, New Mexico, New York, North Carolina, Ohio, Oklahoma, Oregon, Pennsylvania, South Carolina, South Dakota, Tennessee, Texas, Utah, Vermont, Virginia, Washington, West Virginia, Wisconsin, Wyoming, Alberta, British Columbia (including Vancouver Island), Manitoba, Newfoundland, Nova Scotia, Ontario, Saskatchewan, Yukon, Bahama Islands

<u>Winters</u>: Throughout Mexico, except extreme southern. (May also winter in Panama.)

Rufous

Female Rufous.
(Juveniles are similar.)

<u>Specifications</u>: One wing of males averages 40.3 mm; females 44.4 mm. Male weights average 3.22 g; females 3.41 g. Notice that females are larger than males.

The Rufous is more widely distributed than any other hummingbird in North America. This bird has been confirmed in forty-seven American states, (North Dakota and Rhode Island have not verified a Rufous), eight Canadian provinces/territories and twenty-two of Mexico's thirty-two states. A Rufous also holds the long distance hummingbird flight record, plus the record for a long trip with the shortest elapsed time between banding and recapture: 747 miles (1,195 km) in 15 days. (For detailed long distance flight data, see below). Another distinguishing feature about this hummingbird is that it breeds farther north than any other hummingbird in the world.

149

A Rufous in action, often described as feisty, suggests this bird's size-to-weight ratio may be nearly optimal, at least among North American hummingbirds. The Rufous' wing loading, the amount of the bird's weight lifted by each square centimeter of its wing area, apparently gives this hummer an advantage in maneuverability (Feinsinger 1988). Although no wind tunnel tests have been conducted on the majority of hummingbirds, the fact that this bird outflies all other North American hummingbirds suggests that Rufous is the speed king. The Rufous is so superior in flight over other hummingbirds that he has been "jailed" for "aggressiveness" at the Arizona-Sonora Desert Museum near Tucson. There the Rufous is isolated in a cage away from the aviary's ten to twelve less endowed southwestern hummingbirds.

When a Rufous pursues another bird, he can't help looking like a show-off, simply because of his design. In the U.S. Navy, Rufous hummingbirds would be honored as Top Guns. To jail such a creature is like breaking Babe Ruth's bat because he hit so well, or letting air out of an Indy 500 winner's tires because he was too fast, or taking a hacksaw to the wings of a fighter pilot's plane because he was too good. The San Diego zoo solved their Rufous problem in a different way.

Denise Gillen, a senior bird keeper known as Mother Hummer at the San Diego Zoo, said their experience with the Rufous was the same as the Arizona-Sonora Desert Museum's, but they refused to isolate it from other hummers. Gillen added, however, that the little bird seemed so restless, it was in flight "nearly all of the time." A series of Rufous hummingbirds, none of which bred in the zoo, died within six months after they were confined. Subsequently, San Diego Zoo officials have elected to not confine Rufous hummingbirds in their aviary until zoo managers find a caging system compatible with this hummingbird's persona.

The Rufous migration route from Mexico to Alaska is the longest of any North American hummingbird. In proportion to size, the Rufous makes the longest migration of any bird in the world (Johnsgard 1983; Calder 1987).

It is possible that in late summer and early fall a few Rufous break away from the common migration route leading south out of Alaska and Canada. These few birds, rather than going south, head east across Canada to New-foundland. It is possible that from there these few birds turn south, down the east coast to Florida and the Bahamas, and eventually back to Mexico. Such a migration route, from its start in Mexico, would cover 11,000–11,500 miles. Time may prove these hummingbirds to be not only champion travelers among hummingbirds, but the world champion travelers among all birds.

If in the future we ascertain that a few of these hummingbirds do travel

Rufous

an average of a thousand miles per month, it could be possible these tiny mites stop traveling only long enough to breed in Alaska, western Canada, and the northwestern United States. The example of the San Diego Zoo's restless Rufous dying within six months may indicate that being constantly on the move is important to this hummingbird's survival.

To date, nine Rufous that had bands placed on their little legs have been recaptured . . . over one third of the hummingbirds recaptured across a state line from where they were banded. Their verified flights are:

1,733 miles (2,773 km) from Vista Verde Ranch, near Clark, Colorado, August 1991, recaptured Yes Bay, Alaska, June 1993 (adult female).

1,414 miles (2,262 km) banded Ramsey Canyon September 1991; recovered near Mt. Saint Helens, Washington, May 1992.

1,090 miles (1,744 km) from Gothic, Colorado, July 1990; recovered on an island east of Nanaimo, Vancouver Island, Canada, June 1991 (female). (Sticky pine pitch covered some of this bird's feathers, hindering its ability to fly. The bird died during cleaning.)

1,030 miles (1,648 km) banded in Gothic, Colorado, July 1991; recovered April 1992 on the Lumi Reservation west of Bellingham, Washington (female).

747 miles (1,195 km), banded at Swan Lake, Montana, July 25, 1988; recaptured August 9, 1988, at Gothic, Colorado (young female).

644 miles (1,030 km): California to Oregon.

562 miles (899 km) Pensacola, Florida, December 1992 to Springfield, Missouri, November 1993 (adult female).

422 miles (675 km): a juvenile banded August 16, 1990 by Dr. Bill Calder north of Silver City, New Mexico. The bird was recovered eleven months and twelve days later, near Gothic, Colorado. Considering that it was banded during fall migration, and was almost certainly heading south, it seems logical to presume this Rufous flew a circular route around our western mountain range to get from New Mexico to Colorado. If the bird never entered Mexico during the winter of 1990–1991, which is unlikely, the minimum distance this hummingbird could have flown between banding in 1990 and recovery in 1991 was approximately 2,760 miles (4,416 km).

The ninth rufous was an adult male banded in July of 1988 at Swan Lake, Montana. Two years later, the hummer was recaptured 40 miles (64 km) away, near Bigfork, Montana. Considering Montana winters, it is likely this bird also flew a long circular route.

The longevity record for a Rufous is a 6 year old female, last captured at Swan Lake, Montana, in 1991.

The Rufous hummingbird apparently also makes hops across open water, since it is listed on checklists in the Bahama Islands.

This little hummer is one of the first to migrate north, entering southern California as early as January. With so many miles to cover, it seems logical the Rufous would travel early.

Rufous reports east of the Mississippi have caused speculation as to whether the bird is expanding its range or has been there all along. Some think this hummingbird is being observed for the first time in new places due to the increasing popularity of backyard feeders. However, reports of Rufous east of the Mississippi date back to 1909, with numerous sightings since (Conway & Drennan 1979; *Atlanta Journal and Constitution* 1990). I'm inclined to think the bird has been flying these areas all along, and backyard feeders simply make sighting it easier.

A Rufous characteristic I have noticed is that when this bird flies, its flight is most often no nonsense and arrow straight, whereas other hummingbirds seem to jink left and right, or up and down. In that regard, a Rufous flight path reminds me of a laden B-26 (Martin) World War II bomber on a mission. The difference is, when challenged, this bird becomes a nimble, almost unbeatable fighter plane. This master at aerial maneuverability is the only hummer I've seen that does not back away from wasps or bees; in fact, it will sometimes take off in hot pursuit of these insects. This little hummingbird will also pursue just about anything it considers a threat. For example, near Belton, Montana, a forest ranger observed a nesting Rufous dart after an olive-backed thrush so vigorously the thrush squawked and withdrew; a chipmunk searching for huckleberries below the brooding hummer's nest scampered away, squealing, from the female Rufous' "attack" (DuBois 1938). And it's difficult not to root for the Rufous when it faces and refuses to yield to a large Blue-throated or Magnificent hummingbird, creating a David and Goliath scene. When feeding at yellow-bellied sapsucker holes, this little bird even battles for feeding rights in the face of the hole's "owner". During a photographing session I encountered a "tailless" young male among a gaggle of Broad-tails jockeying for feeding rights at a feeder. Not giving an inch, the little bird was a ludicrous sight. I was amazed that he even managed to fly. But fly he did, and agilely enough to own the airspace surrounding the feeder. His tailless agility caused me to wonder if hummingbird tailfeathers aren't used more as semophoric communications emblems than flight devices. (Dr. Bill Baltosser also suspects that may be true.)

The Rufous is the only known hummingbird that goes into torpor at night, even though it is "fat" with high energy reserves. Other hummingbirds go into torpor only as an emergency measure, when energy reserves become dangerously low. By going into torpor when their reserves are not low, Rufous hummingbirds conserve energy at a rate exceeding most hummers. In other words, these little birds live energy efficient lives. If they were in the automobile world, they would be fuel mileage champions. Also, it has been observed that this bird avoids foraging in areas where flowers are sparse, favoring instead places where flowers are thick (Hixon & Carpenter 1988). This may explain why a Rufous dominates feeders, which represent rich foraging. In the southwest during late summer and early fall, one Rufous often defends one nectar-producing century plant for several days running. Between feedings, the bird perches atop a plant rich in nectar and eyes his surroundings for potential intruders.

The three most common hummingbirds in North America, the Rufous, Ruby-throated, and Black-chinned, are close in size and weight. These three are also the number one, two, and three champions in distance and/or area covered throughout the year. In size, the Rufous is between the smaller Ruby-throated and the larger Black-chinned, reenforcing my thought that this bird's anatomical design may be optimal for North American humming-birds. Rufous often appear larger than their measurements authenticate. This misleading appearance may result from an illusion stemming from their coloration.

Rufous rank twelfth in size among sixteen hummingbirds that breed in the United States or Canada.

The Rufous is difficult to separate from Allen's hummingbirds when identifying in the field, especially females and immatures. Generally, mature males have bright Rufous sides *and* bright orange backs. By contrast, mature male Allen's hummingbirds have metallic green backs and heads. Female and immature Rufous and Allen's are so similar, an expert is needed for accurate identification.

As for the Rufous jailed in the Arizona-Sonora Desert Museum near Tucson, I would be more comfortable if a sign on his bars proclaimed: "World's greatest hummingbird."

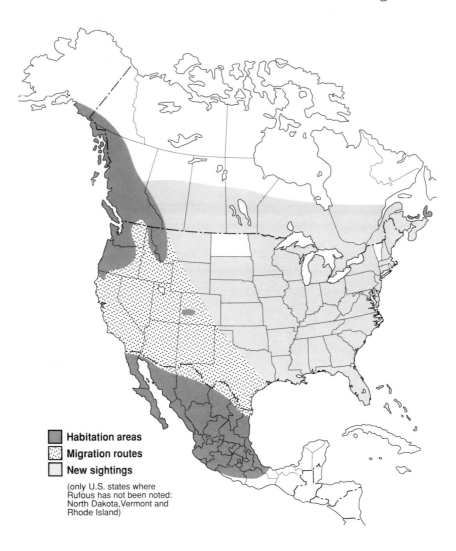

Habitation areas
Migration routes
New sightings

(only U.S. states where
Rufous has not been noted:
North Dakota, Vermont and
Rhode Island)

Rufous hummingbird breeding and wintering range. Stippling depicts probable migration routes.

VIOLET-CROWNED HUMMINGBIRD
Amazilia violiceps

Male Violet-crowned

<u>Where found</u>: Arizona, California (south), New Mexico (south), Texas (west)

<u>Winters</u>: Mexico (Common around Guadalajara)

<u>Specifications</u>: One side of a male's wing averages 57 mm; females 54.9 mm. Male weights average 5.78 g; females 5.19 g

    The Violet-crowned is a rare visitor to the United States. It is also the third largest hummingbird that visits the U.S., ranking below the Magnificent. This bird is easy to identify because it has the lightest (whitest) undersides of any North American species. The Violet-crowned is one of the few hummingbirds where both male and female are almost identical in color-

Violet-crowned

Female Violet-crowned

ation. Only slight differences occur in crown coloring, with the male's crown a shade more brilliant violet than the female's.

This hummingbird breeds fairly regularly but in small numbers in Guadalupe Canyon of southeast Arizona and southwest New Mexico. It seems to be expanding its range, with a fair population in Patagonia, Arizona, and around the Patagonia-Sonoita Creek Sanctuary. One apparently overwintered in Tucson, since it came to a feeder from late November through late February (American Birds 25:610). The Violet-crowned is also found in Arizona's Chiricahua mountains in summer, as well as the Huachucas and lower parts of Ramsey Canyon. Violet-crowneds are usually found at elevations below 5,000 feet beginning in late June. Occasionally it is spotted in Tucson, and once in a while drifts as far north as Phoenix.

Like most hummingbirds, the Violet-crowned has no song, but it does have a distinctive alarm call. Bill Baltosser describes this hummingbird's alarm voice as a ticking sound similar to the sound of quarter-inch steel balls rattling against one another in one's hand.

To date, not a single banded Violet-crowned has been recovered away from its banding site.

Of the sixteen breeding species, the Violet-crowned ranks third in size.

Violet-crowned

Violet-crowned hummingbird breeding and residential range.

Habitation areas
New sightings

WHITE-EARED HUMMINGBIRD
Hylocharis leucotis

Male White-eared

<u>Where found</u>: Texas, New Mexico, and Arizona

<u>Winters</u>: Mountains throughout Mexico, except Baja

<u>Specifications</u>: One side of wing on males averages 55.3 mm; females average 51.9 mm. Weight of average male is 3.6 g; females 3.2 g

The White-eared is a rare hummingbird in the United States. Males are not only brightly colored, but their outer tail feathers are tipped with white. The Blue-throated male is the only other North American male hummingbird with white-tipped tail feathers.

White-eared hummingbirds are generally high tropical mountain birds. Their nests have been found from elevations varying between 3,000 feet at Tepic, Nayarit, Mexico, and on the Urique River at the bottom of the

160

White-eared

Juvenile male.
(White-eared female almost identical.)

Barranca del Cobre, to 10,500 feet on Mount Mohinora, Chihuahua, Mexico (near Batopilas). In the mountains of northwest Mexico, above 5,000 feet, the White-eared is more common than any other hummingbird. One May, on the paint-brush beds at 10,000 feet on the slopes of Mount Mohinora, White-eared hummingbirds outnumbered Broad-bills, Blue-throated, and Magnificents put together (Moore 1939).

In Texas' Chisos Mountains of Big Bend, White-eared hummingbirds have been recorded from April 27 to August 13, which is enough time to breed. In Arizona's Chiricahua Mountains (Cave Creek Canyon) and Huachuca Mountains (Ramsey Canyon), the birds have been seen between June 9 and August 14. In southwest New Mexico's Animas Mountains, they have been noted in June and July.

The White-eared is a rare North American breeder. Carrol Peabody of Tucson claims this hummingbird nests as far north as near Summerhaven Lodge on Tucson's 9,225-foot Mt. Lemmon. New White-eared nests are often constructed on the remains of old ones.

The White-eared is considered to be a generalist forager, feeding from a wide variety of different sized flowers at differing heights (Lyon 1976). When feeding, the bird "pumps" its tail up and down. In an area shared with larger Magnificents and Blue-throateds, the smaller (and consequently more maneuverable) White-eared dominates, often pursuing a rival until completely out of a feeding area. In spite of their pugnaciousness, White-eareds were the shyest of four species. At Rancho Batel, in southeastern Sinaloa, Mexico, Calliope, Broad-tailed, and Margaret hummingbirds tolerated movie photography as near as six feet. However, White-eared hummers moved to the opposite side of their feeding bush when the camera began operating, or departed entirely (Moore, 1939).

As with other tropical hummingbirds that visit the southern fringes of the United States, White-eared hummingbirds are more colorful than non-tropical hummers. No banded White-eared has ever been recovered away from its banding site.

Of the sixteen breeding species, the White-eared ranks fifth in size.

■ Habitation areas
□ New sightings

White-eared hummingbird breeding and residential range.

How to Photograph Hummingbirds

Why photograph hummingbirds? Because it provides a classroom for learning the intimate habits and minds of these charming birds. For example, when I used a camera triggered by a hummingbird moving into focus, I was surprised at how quickly the birds learned where the invisible tripping point was. Once a bird triggered my camera, and its flash, the bird became expert at avoiding that tiny bit of airspace when it returned to the feeder near the camera. On its next visit a bird previously "flashed" would hover only millimeters to one side of that magic camera-tripping spot. Just short of the focus point, the hummingbird would turn its head sideways toward the feeder, then extend its tongue the maximum, and feed. This happened with nearly every species I filmed, except for a female Black-chinned.

After this hummingbird set off my camera, she simply backed off six inches or so, hovered a moment, then moved precisely into that focus point again. The camera and flash fired. Again she backed away a few inches, paused a moment, and again flew deliberately into the camera's triggering point. This female Black-chinned repeated her camera-tripping sortie five successive times, apparently amused with the camera's flash. (My flash units are set at only 1/64 power, and therefore make little more than a wink.)

When I film where there is a mixture of two or more species of hummingbirds coming to the feeder, I hunker under camouflage material over the instrument, arming it to photograph only the species I want. Those long sessions at the camera educated my ears to the different wing sounds of each species. The Rufous wing sound is that of a finely tuned, smooth running, high performance race engine. When the Rufous changes its wing pitch to accelerate or do other maneuvers, the change in its wing sound is smooth as velvet. By contrast, the humming sound of other species' wings are jerky, sounding more like an ordinary, lower performance engine.

Filming these little birds in flight turned out to be more difficult and require more equipment than I anticipated. To capture these little critters in flight it takes, at a minimum, four flash units (three on the bird and one for background), two tri-pods, a background stand (tripods can be reduced to one by welding up a fixture for attaching the background flash to the background stand), and, of course, a camera and lens. All of my photographs are of wild, unconfined birds. Some hummingbird photos show birds' wingtips and/or tail feathers frayed or broken because the birds were held in a cage or tent for photographing. (Sometimes these broken feathers are explained away as "molting".) In my view, a free-flying wild bird has, along with intact feathers, a soul and spirit that is also intact. An intact soul and spirit adds to the vitality of a hummingbird's film image.

In 1928 photographer Margaret Bodine of Maine described hummingbird photography as "sufficiently difficult to arouse one's sporting instinct" (Bodine 1928). Considering that Ms. Bodine photographed hummingbirds without benefit of flash equipment, her task was daunting, but even with modern strobes, filming hummingbirds remains sporty.

I began my first hummingbird photo session with hardly a break from three months of eagle filming. I'd been told that eagles were the most difficult bird to film, yet I found the project relatively easy. Therefore, I reasoned, "I'll do this hummingbird piece, including photos, in an afternoon and move on to writing a third eagle book." Since that fateful conclusion, I have been forced to recognize that hummingbirds are birds of a different feather in more ways than one. That afternoon has stretched into its second year, my hummingbird photo learning curve continues to climb, and the eagle book remains in progress, but on hold. The hummingbird challenge has been both testy and humbling.

When I filmed eagles, I expected, and got, finished photographs closely matching what I saw in the viewfinder. In other words, eagle images were reasonably predictable. Hummingbird film produced one surprise after another. Eagles soared on more or less fixed wings and remained right side up. With hummingbirds, there was no telling in what position a snap of the camera might record their wings; where I thought I had filmed the little rascals flying right side up, my film came back with images of semi-inverted hummingbirds, sometimes in hilarious positions. There was no predicting which way their graceful beak was likely to be pointing. Tail feather configurations held further surprises. One roll of film I especially recall.

I had modified a feeder in the hope of getting photographs of hummingbirds hovering. I used a camera that can be instructed to fire automatically the instant a hummingbird had moved into perfect focus. After a roll of film had run, I was satisfied that my feeder

Hummingbird feeding in flight.

modification was nearly perfect. While the film was out for processing I imagined frames of beautifully hovering hummingbirds . . . birds hovering in level flight as they sipped from a feeder. When the film came back, every frame was of hummingbirds on their sides, in a ninety-degree bank, with wings and tail feathers in as many positions and shapes as there are people's faces, while their beaks were implanted in the feeder's port.

A study of these photos revealed that the birds began slurping sugar water while they were still in steeply banked flight. It was obvious that a split second before the birds roll into level flight, they insert their beaks into a feeding port and get two or three slurps as they roll from banked flight to level flight. The maneuver conserves the bird's energy because it allows them to do two things at once, both happening too fast for human eyes to catch. The camera fired automatically when it sensed a bird in focus, not caring whether the bird was hovering or in a steep bank. After adjusting the camera's focus point, I got the hovering photos I wanted. Believing I had hummingbird photog-

167

raphy figured out, I drove 440 miles to western Oklahoma for pictures of Ruby-throats. I was in for another surprise.

In late May I found a farm near Sayre, Oklahoma, with everything hummingbirds need—flowers, trees, water, and insects. Feeders had been put up there for the past thirty years. After watching feeder traffic, I estimated the farm's hummingbird population at about thirty, evenly split between Ruby-throats and Black-chins. (Birdwatchers from other parts of Oklahoma insist there are no Ruby-throats or Black-chins in the western part of their state, but I produced a photo of a Ruby-throated and a Black-chinned feeding together in western Oklahoma.) A trip to photograph hummingbirds taught me that western Oklahoma counties probably are the east-west dividing line for these two species. Throughout those western counties I saw an overlapping population of Ruby-throats and Black-chins. My first evening at the farm, after my cameras were set, the surprise occurred.

Ellie Womack, hummingbird bander at Grove, in eastern Oklahoma, had informed me of a span of time, at least in Oklahoma, when Ruby-throated hummingbirds cease feeder visits. The interruption lasts from ten days to two weeks. At the farm where I had set my cameras, there were Ruby-throats in the morning, the last day of May. By evening, there were none to be seen among the Black-chins. (In Ohio, Sara Jean Peters reports this same Ruby-throated disappearance from feeders in early June (Peters 1991).)

No one's certain why Ruby-throats shut down on feeder visits. Since their disappearance coincides closely with nesting season, there may be a connection. Or a flower, or flowers, may bloom at May's end which the birds prefer over feeders. The Black-chins continued using the feeders in the absence of their cousins. Not needing Black-chinned film, I phoned Ellie, 300 miles to the east, to see if the Ruby-throated feeding phenomenon had struck in Grove.

She said that her Ruby-throats had also abandoned her twenty feeders. She further explained that when the feeder shutdown ends, the birds return as suddenly as they disappeared. Because there are no Black-chins at Grove, air there empties of hummingbirds when the Ruby-throats quit. Sayre, near the farm where I planned to film, is a nice town with friendly people and a delightful little golf course. However, I didn't have time to wait two weeks for the Ruby-throats to return. Feeling I had lost a couple of days to unproductive travel I too abandoned the farm's hummingbird feeders and returned to Albuquerque. There, another hummingbird photo surprise came about.

In Albuquerque I used for the first time a Pentax 6×7 camera to film hummers. This camera I fired manually, well after the hummers had rotated, stabilized in hover, and were sipping from a feeder. The surprise came when my film showed every frame with birds disconnected from the feeder by two or three inches and roaring away. Each bird had moved out of focus. What had happened was this. The Pentax is a large, single-lens reflex camera (2¼″ by 2¾″ negative) with a correspondingly large mirror. When I fired the camera, two events happened in rapid sequence. First, the mirror pivoted up out of the way and slapped against its stops. Then the shutter and flash fired. Mirror slap came a split second before shutter and flash operation. The instant the mirror slapped, the hummingbird jerked away, and was out of focus when the shutter and flash fired. Some of the bird's escape configurations were hilarious, such as one with beak pointing earthward and wings raked backward, like a jet fighter.

Mirror slap prior to shutter operation is a potential problem with any medium-to-large format, single-lens reflex camera. The problem is solved by locking the mirror in its "up" position prior to each photograph. Mirror slap can sometimes be turned to the photographer's advantage.

Unusual hummingbird flight regimens can present interesting images. These photos, properly prefocused and framed, can be achieved by preplanning mirror slap. For example, with a Mamiya 645 series camera, mirror slap and shutter operation can be used to capture a hummingbird poised in midair. It happens in this sequence: The mirror slap causes the bird to begin backing away from the feeder to escape; then the shutter and flash fire, capturing the bird in midair, away from the feeder but not yet out of focus. Often droplets of sugar water are suspended in front of a beak that was hastily withdrawn. Anticipating this action, I frame and prefocus to capture the action flow. These photos make nice enlargements because it is easy to crop the feeder out of the picture and isolate an in-flight hummingbird, suspended alone in mid-air.

The 35mm SLR camera mirrors are so small they pivot up and slap faster than most hummingbirds can react before the shutter freezes them on film. However, the smaller (quicker) hummingbirds can react to mirror slap and move out of the frame ahead of the shutter. Between-the-lens shutters are so well flash synchronized that they avoid the problem of focal plane-shutter-mirror combinations. Through events such as these I constantly refine my hummingbird photography, which is a lot like filming rainbows and clouds—no two pictures are alike.

How to Photograph Hummingbirds

Harold Edgerton developed the modern strobe flash during the late 1920s and early 1930s (Edgerton 1987). Applying his invention, Edgerton was first to film hummingbirds via stroboscopic light, also known as strobe or speedlight (Edgerton 1947). Edgerton's pictures were made with units that had flash durations (speeds) of one three-thousandths ($\frac{1}{3,000}$) of a second. It is a safe bet that most of the important hummingbird photographs seen today are taken with improved versions of the strobe Edgerton invented.

By combining his strobe with a modified movie camera, Edgerton established that a hovering female Ruby-throated hummingbird beats its wings 55 beats per second. (Edgerton's data was collected in Holderness, New Hampshire, at an altitude of 584 feet and an average temperature of 73° F. Males will have a slightly faster wingbeat because they are smaller. In 1960 Crawford Greenewalt calculated a female Ruby-throat at 53 beats/second.) Fifty-three to 55 beats a second produces a maximum tip speed, the fastest moving part of a bird wing, of about 20 mph. These speeds present unique photo problems.

Hummingbird wings are rigid from their ball-jointed shoulders out to their tips. Feathers, of course, are flexible. Edgerton's high-speed photographs revealed that a hovering hummingbird treads air. The stiff-winged hummer moves its wings back and forth, in the same way human swimmers tread water by moving arms and hands back and forth. As the bird's wing gyrates back and forth, it pivots on its leading edge via a ball joint in the bird's shoulder. This pivoting feature allows the generation of lift on both forward and backward strokes. This wing motion is fairly level with the ground, as opposed to the up-and-down strokes of conventional birds. Strangely, a hummingbird's wing maintains a constant beat frequency (Greenewalt 1960b). For differing flight regimens, from hover to cross-country cruising and all others between, the bird simply changes the pitch of its wing, to take advantage of translational lift, rather than alter its beat frequency. Each species has different wingbeats per second; the larger the wing, the slower it beats, and vice versa. The arc through which a hummingbird's wing moves is a little more than 90 degrees. During hover, the wingbeat arc swings through only about 15 to 25 degrees.

I found information regarding freezing hummingbird wings via flash photography in a July 1963 *National Geographic* article by Crawford Greenewalt, then president of the DuPont company. Greenewalt wrote that to photograph hummingbirds he used specially made flash equipment generating a pulse of 30-millionths of a second. "Millionths of a second" intimidated me to the point where I reckoned hummingbird photography might be beyond my reach. Then I realized that the fraction thirty-millionths reduces to a mere $\frac{1}{33,333}$ of a second. Relieved, I discovered such a flash could be made economically at home by following instructions in the unselfish Edgerton's book, *Electronic Flash, Strobe*. Before investing time in a flash fabrication project, I checked specifications on commercially produced flash units I owned.

Most commercial flash units pulse at around $\frac{1}{5,000}$ of a second. I discovered it was possible to shorten the pulse of any variable power flash by reducing output to its minimum. Output of Vivitar's #283 flash, combined with a Vari-power, can be reduced to $\frac{1}{64}$. At $\frac{1}{64}$ power, the 283 pulsed at $\frac{1}{30,000}$ of a second. That discovery raised my hopes for successful hummingbird photography. As it was winter, and no hummingbirds were near Albuquerque, I devised a plan to test the 283's $\frac{1}{64}$ flash duration against simulated hummingbird wing speeds.

One November night I compared Ruby-throated wing tip speeds to tip speeds of a two-speed electric fan. Calculations included the fan's rpm and blade circumference. When my fan was set on low speed, the tips of its blades were very near Ruby-throated hummingbird wing tip speeds. A simple test would determine if my figures were reasonable. On the leading edge of one of the fan's white blades I stuck a strip of black tape. In a darkened room I set the blades whirring. Repeatedly I flashed the strobe's $\frac{1}{30,000}$ of a second at the fan. Visually, it appeared to freeze the tape's motion. Pictures of the blade would provide an accurate answer. I loaded my camera and exposed a roll of film on the whirling blades.

Photos showed that $\frac{1}{30,000}$ of a second froze the fan's blades to within half an inch of the tips, which move faster than any other segment of the blade. The slight blurred area was so short and negligible I considered it insignificant. The fan-blade test suggested that I had a reasonable chance to freeze hummingbird wings with an off-the-shelf flash. Since the proof is in the pudding, I was anxious to film a real hummingbird. Unless I traveled to Mexico, I'd have to wait until spring for that proof. Then, Amarillo's winterbound Anna's dropped into my lap.

Photos of the Anna's confirmed my fan test. Its wings were, for practical purposes, photographically frozen, with a small exception. At the bird's highest wing speed, midstroke, there was minor blurring at the tips. At slower, fore-and-aft positions, where the wing slows and stops prior to reversing direction, the entire wing, including its tip, was frozen. From that test I estimated the Vivitar 283 was very close to "thirty-millionths of a second," and therefore would freeze the average hummingbird's wing through about 90 percent of its arc. Considering how little I would have to invest in flash equipment, I marched toward hummingbird photography.

As a general rule, the smaller the hummingbird, the faster its wing beat. Lucifer, Allen's, Ruby-throated, and Calliope are the smallest North American hummingbirds (Johnsgard 1983), and therefore the most challenging to photograph. Although only slightly smaller than Ruby-throateds, Lucifers and Allen's require a flash faster than $1/30,000$ of a second to freeze wing action throughout wing travel. At the same time, since minor blurring occurs only at the wing tips during mid-stroke, I consider the problem to be unimportant. A flash at $1/30,000$ of a second stops these smaller bird's wings through the slower parts of their arc, and produces sharp photographs. (Calliope humming-birds are slightly larger than Ruby-throateds, and therefore easier to film). Even ordinary flash units, those with speeds as slow as $1/5,000$ of a second, will freeze extreme fore and aft phases of any hummingbird wingbeat, where wings slow and stop prior to reversing direction. Rules, then, for a fixed duration flash in hummingbird photography are: the smaller the hummingbird, the faster its wings beat, and vice versa; slower wingbeats increase the length of travel that will be frozen, and vice versa; photos of wings near their fore or aft reversal points are more likely to freeze action.

In the 1960s and 1970s Honeywell made flash units with pulses of $1/50,000$ to $1/70,000$ of a second. These older strobes can be found at garage sales and flea markets. The only other commercial flash I know of with speeds that fast is Minolta's 5200i. This unit is advertised as capable of $1/50,000$ of a second, but can be used only on certain Minolta cameras. Other flashes to consider, which will work with most any camera, are the Nissin 5000GT, advertised as $1/30,000$ of a second, and Metz's 45CT, advertised as capable of $1/25,000$ of a second.

At 1/64 power, light transmitted by a Vivitar 283 is only a wink. Great for not frightening hummingbirds. In bright sunlight, they hardly give the bird notice. But a wink of light casts very little illumination. To boost illumination, I used three flash units. To facilitate camera and flash mountings I fashioned a rack that held camera and flash units on one tripod. Although multiple flash units increased my light output to an acceptable level, at the same time they introduced a dilemma that took months to solve.

Mass-produced flash units are not represented as precise, scientific instruments Individual units may have pulse beginnings that vary by a few milliseconds from one flash to the next. These lagging (or leading) out-of-sync pulses also generate multiple, unsynchronized illuminations. Multiple illuminations make multiple images, which causes blurring of hummingbird wings. A lab equipped with precision instruments can measure one flash against another until matching units are found. Considering the bother and expense of that option, I returned to my fan blade test.

By flashing the blades, preferably in darkness, a fairly close match can be found among multiple flash units by sight. Final testing for a matched set can be done via film. When I had a matched set that froze fan blades, and hummingbird wings, that set was tagged and numbered. Even though once in a while wings blur, I enjoy the fact that 1/30,000 of a second is available, reasonably priced, and stops the average hummingbird's wing through a wide range of its stroke. (Once you have a matched set, protect it against temperature extremes, otherwise their synchronization may be lost.)

My flash units are set with one at top left of the lens, one top right, and one at bottom center. I elevated the left and right units a couple of inches above the lens' center line and aimed them slightly downward, to the focus point. Three units create a crude "ring" flash. To be certain of lighting gorgets on the male birds, light from a flash must strike the gorget at a downward angle of 20 degrees or more. Also, light must be inside of a 20-degree angle either side of center, measured from the bird. Put another way, gorget lighting has a total corridor of 40 degrees, or 20 degrees each side of center, from the bird. (I am grateful to Carroll Peabody of Tucson, who has filmed hummingbirds over fifty years, for this information.)

One further refinement I apply is to place the bottom flash back far enough to reduce its output by one stop compared with the total of the two left and right units. The bottom flash concentrates on hummingbird undersides, which are generally lighter in color and therefore easily overexposed on film. Reducing the bottom flash's lighting captures greater feather detail and truer colors of hummingbird bellies.

To gain enough light for one more stop I sometimes fit each flash with a telephoto filter that focuses light into a tighter, more intense pattern. For consistent light output, rapid recycling, and to eliminate the cost of replacing twelve batteries each day, I use 110 power converters. In the field I rely on a small generator and a long extension cord.

A couple of more things to remember in photographing these little

Author with photo setup.

birds: molting generally occurs just prior to each species' breeding season. For photo purposes, then, the best-groomed feathers adorn a bird just before its nesting season. During spring migration the more colorful males usually arrive a week or so ahead of the females, so for that week your feeder traffic will be colorful. Consider also behavioral effects caused by the birds' daytime body temperature, as high as 109° F. At that temperature the little birds burn energy at such a rapid clip nature has given them a way to conserve reserves in order for them to make it through the night. This event opens more photo opportunities.

Nightfall metabolic rates of hummingbirds drop as much as 90 percent. At that reduced rate, depending on energy reserves, the birds sometimes go into a diurnal state called torpor. In torpor the bird's body temperature drops to 65° F, which lowers its energy requirements to about 10 percent of normal. To make it through the night, hummingbirds stock up on nourishment near sundown. For this reason, photo opportunities at a feeder increase from just before sundown to dusk. A corresponding increase in traffic occurs just after sunrise when the bird's body temperature is returning to normal and they zip to feeders for nourishment. Through two different sunrise periods I timed Black-chinned feeder trips. A male averaged eleven feeder visits an hour, beginning 15 minutes before sunrise. That averages to a trip every 5.5 minutes. An hour after sunrise, feeder visits dropped dramatically. During the day individual hummers fed at intervals varying from 20 to 30 minutes. The little birds also seemed to respond to approaching thunderstorms or weather changes by crowding around feeders, apparently to take on enough energy to last through the storm. If the rain is a cold rain, a rain too uncomfortable for them to fly in and/or lasting an hour or more, they may occasionally take refuge in trees or shrubs and go into a semi-torpid state. In this semi torpid state they are easy to photograph as they sit perched in cold wind and rain. Keeping photo equipment and photographer dry may not be so easy.

By selecting the right combination of film speed, shutter speed, ambient sunlight and flash power you can use natural backgrounds, including the sky, and eliminate the midnight black seen in many hummingbird photo backgrounds. Because this system utilizes two light sources, ghosting can occur and may require tests to eliminate. I also use either natural green vegetation backgrounds or sky with patches of white clouds. If none of these backgrounds is feasible, I use a portable backdrop suspended on a stand built of 1 inch water pipe. This background can have shadows.

If there is a breeze, hummingbirds prefer facing into it when they feed. By using a small fan or blower, you can control which way they face relative to your lens by directing air across your photo's frame. At one time it seemed reasonable to me that air flowing across the hovering hummingbird would slow its wing beat, making photography easier. That idea unraveled when I learned that Crawford Greenewalt made high-speed movies of a female Ruby-throated in a wind tunnel during the 1950s (Greenewalt 1960b). The tunnel contained a feeder positioned in a way that made the hummingbird fly upstream to reach the food source. Greenewalt discovered that regardless of wind speed, which he varied from zero to 30 mph, the Ruby-throat's wingbeat frequency changed no more than 5 percent from its normal 53 to 55 beats a second rate. A "constant beat wing" operates essentially the way an aircraft's "constant speed propeller" operates, by changing pitch angle to compensate for differing flight speeds and power loadings. Although a stream of air flowing across a feeder won't slow the bird's wingbeat, the moving air will produce a variety of wing pitches, which for photography will generate an array of interesting wing (and tail and body) configurations.

There are as many different opinions about which camera and lens to use for hummingbirds as there are photographers. I use a camera equipped with a macro lens and a computerized back that allows me to preselect a focus point. Each time a hummingbird invades that prefocused point, the bird's focused image causes the camera to fire. It's called focus priority. Focus priority not only allows me to avoid being an intruder and possibly interfering with the hummer's territory, it also frees me from slaving over a camera for long periods. I can be at a movie, changing oil in the car, or lolling on a Mexican beach . . . a bird takes its own picture the instant it enters the camera's preselected focus point. One minor drawback to focus priority is that if a wasp, bee, or dandelion seed floats in and breaches the focus point, the camera fires. Hands and fingers making camera adjustments are also photographed by focus priority when one fails to disarm the camera before making framing changes. *Note*: An inherent problem with focus priority is that the camera's mirror cannot be locked up. Some brands of cameras have a focus priority/mirror combination that operates too slowly to fire the camera quickly enough before the bird moves out of focus, or out of center frame.

For prefocusing and framing I use a fake hummingbird fashioned from a wooden spring-type clothespin fitted with cardboard "wings." A toothpick clamped in the clothespin's jaws represents the bird's bill. I call this device a Spring-breasted Pine Beak, or *Clotheus springus*.

If you have an older camera with a motor drive or winder, you can come close to achieving focus priority by using an infra-red triggering device in the same way that a prefocused point will cause a bird to fire your camera.

Incidentally, photo opportunities increase if you maintain your photo feeder at no richer than a one-to-four sugar-water ratio. That mixture is not only healthful for the birds, it also keeps them returning to a feeder more often than mixtures with higher sugar concentrations. In fact, hummingbird activity increases at feeders that have lower sugar concentrations (Stromberg & Johnson 1990). With leaner sugar mixtures the birds not only feed more often, they also stay at the feeder longer and move from port to port. For those reasons, I use a five-to-one mixture when filming hummingbirds.

An environment that includes gnat swarms near a feeder, and within camera range, increases photo opportunities. When I travel during the warm months. I put out a feeder and set up to photograph wherever I camp. Near the beach south of Todos Santos, Baja, a male Anna's was feeding and I was photographing within a day after I put up a feeder in mid-January.

After years of filming these interesting little birds I have concluded that one reason they remain so difficult to film is that they spend their lives as fulltime hummingbirds, while, as members of modern society, we are able to be hummingbird photographers only part-time.

Hummer Trivia

There are more than 330 known species of hummingbirds (*Trochilidae*). That number ranks *Trochilidae* as the second highest species count among the world's birds. (Flycatchers, *Tyrannidae*, rank first.) In all the world, hummingbirds have been found only in North, Central, and South America. Ecuador, with 150 hummingbird species, probably has more of these birds than any other single area.

Hummingbirds of North America
24 species total. Eleven are important breeders; 5 are minor breeders.

Hummingbirds that breed in the United States and Canada:
 Allen's *Selasphorus sasin*
 Anna's *Calypte anna*
 Berylline *Amazilia beryllina* (rare breeder in extreme SE Arizona)
 Black-chinned *Archilochus alexandri*
 Blue-throated *Lampornis clemenciae*
 Broad-billed *Cynanthus latirostris*
 Broad-tailed *Selasphorus platycercus*
 Buff-bellied (Fawn-breasted) *Amazilia yucatanensis* (rare breeder in
  Louisana and Texas)
 Calliope *Stellula calliope*
 Costa's *Calypte costae*
 Lucifer *Calothorax Lucifer* (rare breeder in extreme southern Arizona, southern New Mexico, SW Texas)
 Magnificent *Eugenes fulgens*
 Ruby-throated *Archilochus colubris*
 Rufous *Selasphorus rufus*
 Violet-crowned *Amazilia violiceps* (rare breeder in extreme
  southern Arizona and New Mexico)
 White-eared *Hylocharis leucotis* (rare breeder in SE Arizona)

Rare, casual, or accidental hummingbirds of North America
 Antillean Crested *Orthorhyncus cristatus* (one U.S. record, Galveston Island, Texas, February 1, 1967)

Bahama Woodstar *Calliphlox Evelynae* (accidental in extreme southern Florida)

Cuban Emerald *Chlorostilbon ricordii*

Green-breasted Mango *Anthracothorax pervostii* (January 1992, Corpus Christi, Texas)

Green Violet-eared *Colibri thalassinus* (accidental in extreme south Texas, North Carolina, Ontario)

Plain-capped Starthroat *heliomaster Constantii* (accidental in extreme southern Arizona; probably in extreme southern New Mexico)

Rufous-tailed *Amazilia Tzacatl* (accidental in extreme southern Texas)

Xantus' (Black-fronted) *Hylocharis xantusii* (has bred in extreme southern California)

States With the Most Reported Hummingbird Species

1. Texas, with 19, has more species of hummingbirds than any other state in the Union.
2. Arizona has 15 species of hummingbirds. (The Bumblebee, recorded twice in 1896 but not since, is considered a historical species and not included.)
3. New Mexico has 13 species.
4. California has 12 species.
5. Florida, Louisiana, Nevada, and Utah each have 9 species.
6. Arkansas, Colorado, and Oregon each have 7.
7. Alabama, Georgia, Kansas, Mississippi, and Wyoming each have 6 species.
8. Idaho and Montana each have 5.
9. Alaska, Nebraska, North Carolina, Oklahoma, South Dakota, and Washington State each have 4.

Provinces With the Most Reported Hummingbird Species

1. British Columbia, with 7, has more species than any other province. (Vancouver Island has 6.)
2. Ontario has 5 species. (A Green Violet-eared in 1991 was the 5th.)
3. Saskatchewan has 4 hummingbird species.
4. Alberta and Nova Scotia each have 3 species.

Random Notes

Both the largest (Blue-throated) and the smallest (Lucifer) hummingbirds in the United States are found in three states: Arizona, New Mexico, and Texas.

Of North American hummingbirds, the Rufous is known to migrate the greatest distance, flying between Mexico and Alaska.

The largest hummingbird in the world is the Giant hummingbird of the Andes in South America. Weight of the Giant is 20 g, or more than double that of the Blue-throated.

The smallest hummingbird (and bird) known in the world is the Cuban Bee, found on the Isle of Pines in Cuba. This hummingbird is 2¼″ long. Some are smaller than large bumblebees, and are often misidentified as such.

Ruby-throated Hummingbirds Compared to Golden Eagles

One golden eagle primary feather weighs the same as a Ruby-throated hummingbird, 3 grams.

The Ruby-throated hummingbird has a spring-summer wing loading of only one-sixth that of a golden eagle. Ruby-throated wing loading equals 0.15 g per square centimeter, which means that each square centimeter of hummingbird wing must lift 0.15 g.

Golden eagle wing loading equals 0.90 g, which means that each square centimeter of eagle wing must lift 0.90 g—six times more than a Ruby-throated.

For a golden eagle to have a wing loading equal to a Ruby-throated, the eagle would have wings spanning forty-two feet, with no increase in the bird's weight. Put the other way around, if a Ruby-throated had a wing loading equal to a golden eagle's, the hummingbird would have stubby wings, each about as long as the width of a woman's thumb nail. Obviously the hummingbird has an efficient combination of airfoil and wing stroke.

How to Estimate the Number of Hummingbirds You Are Feeding

Hummingbirds eat an amount of 25% sugar content nectar that is equal to about their body weight, daily (Skutch 1973). Determine the weight of the kind of birds you are working with. Then, by weighing the amount of food your birds are consuming, you can compute the number of birds you are feeding. (Ruby-throats weigh 3 g upon arrival at spring breeding grounds, 5.5 g when fattened up for fall migration. A penny minted since 1982 weighs 2.5 g. Nickels minted since 1946 weigh 5 g.) This method of estimating numbers of birds coming to a feeder works best with pan-type models, since they are inherently leakproof. For a scientific use of this method, it would be necessary to establish the evaporation rate during a test period. For practical purposes, evaporation would be of minor importance.

Size Ranking of Male Hummingbirds That Breed in the United States and Canada

(measurements are one wing in mm) (Johnsgard 1983):
1. Blue-throated 76.7 mm (average of 23 males); female is smaller
2. Magnificent 73 mm (average of 31 males); female is smaller
3. Violet-crowned 57 mm (average of 9 males); female is smaller
4. Berylline 55.5 mm (average of 14 males); female is smaller
5. White-eared 55.3 mm (average of 17 males); female is smaller
6. Broad-billed 54.8 mm (average of 8 males); female is smaller (Moore 1939)
7. Buff-bellied 53.8 mm (average of 5 males); female is smaller
8. Anna's 49.7 mm (average of 10 males); female is $\frac{1}{10}$ mm smaller. Anna's is largest west coast hummingbird
9. Broad-tailed 48.4 mm (average of 19 males); female is larger
10. Costa's 44.4 mm (average of 13 males); female is larger
11. Black-chinned 42.7 mm (average of 10 males); female is larger
12. Rufous 40.3 mm (average of 18 males); female is larger
13. Calliope 38.7 mm (average of 46 males); female is larger
14. Ruby-throated 38.5 mm (average of 10 males); female is larger
15. Allen's 37.8 mm (average of 10 *sassin* males); females and *sedentarius* are larger
16. Lucifer 37.6 mm (average of 10 males); female is larger

State and Province/ Territory Species List

United States

Alabama

Number of species reported: 6

Most common: Ruby-throated (breeds statewide)

Rare, casual, accidental: Rufous, Black-chinned, Allen's, Buff-bellied, Anna's

Favored flowers: red buckeye early spring; cardinal flower and jewel-weed in summer; salvia and hibiscus in fall; also mimosa, trumpet vine, hollyhock, columbine, lilies, petunia, impatiens, rhododendron, honeysuckle, coralberry.

Arrival of migrants: Montgomery, Ruby-throated, March 15; earlier south. Rufous, late July. Black-chinned, late July to early August.

Departure of migrants: Montgomery, Ruby-throated October 7; later south. Wintering Black-chins leave mid-April. Wintering Rufous leave late April.

Alaska

Number of species reported: 4

Most common: Rufous (breeds throughout SE coastal region to NW through Prince William Sound)

Rare, casual, accidental: Anna's (mostly SE); Costa's (Anchorage); (only one Ruby-throated recorded, dead on beach 18 miles from St. Michael)

Favored flowers: nasturtium, hanging fuchsia, blueberry, salmon-berry, false azalea, red columbine, Indian paintbrush

Arrival of migrants: First week in May (Rufous)

Departure of migrants: well into October in Anchorage area

Arizona

Number of species reported: 15 (Source: Arizona Bird Committee)

Most common: Black-chinned (breeds throughout in summer); Broad-billed (breeds SE and SW); Anna's (resident south); Magnificent (breeds SE); Rufous (spring/fall migrant);

Broad-tailed (breed SE and north summer); Allen's (migrant SE and SW); Blue-throated (breeds SE); Costa's (breeding resident SW; summer SE and NW); Calliope (migrant); Violet-crowned (occasionally breeds SE); Berylline (occasionally breeds SE)

Rare, casual, accidental: Lucifer (rarely breeds SE); White-eared (SE); Plain-capped Starthroat (SE and SW)

Favored flowers: aloe, agave, lantana, scarlet gilia and penstemons, salvia, betony, desert honeysuckle, hummingbird trumpet, columbine, thistle, Mexican campion, tree tobacco, jacobina, shrimp plant, larkspur

Arrival of migrants: (southeastern Arizona) Costa's mid-January; Broad-tailed, early February; Rufous passes through from mid-February through early May going north, and again beginning in early June going south; Black-chinned, mid-February; Magnificent, March 1; Broad-billed, mid-March; Blue-throated, latter part of March; Calliope begins passing through latter part of March through mid-May going north, and again beginning in mid-July through mid-October going south; Violet-crowned, early May; White-eared mid-May; Berylline, is rare April through September; Lucifer is rare from April through mid-October; Allen's, early July; Anna's, early September.

Departure of migrants: (southeastern Arizona) Anna's, early May, however a few reside year-round; Costa's, late May, with a few returning to winter; Allen's, late August; White-eared, mid-September; Broad-billed, late-September, with a few into November; Calliope, early October; Violet-crowned, mid-October; Blue-throated, mid-October, with a few wintering; Black-chinned, mid-October through December; Broad-tailed, late-October; Rufous, early November, with a few wintering; Magnificent, mid-November, with a few wintering.

Arkansas

Number of species reported: 7

Most common: Ruby-throated (nests statewide)

Rare, casual, accidental: Rufous, Black-chinned, Anna's, Green Violet-eared, Buff-bellied, Magnificent

Favored flowers: coral honeysuckle, red buck-eye, Japanese honeysuckle, scarlet sage

Arrival of migrants: (earliest) second week in March; normal first
week of April

Departure of migrants: normally September to October; latest, first
week of December

California
Number of species reported: 12

Northern California
Number of species reported: 9

Most common: Anna's (resident breeder); Costa's (southwest resident breeder); Black-chinned (resident breeder); Rufous
(migrant); Calliope (migrant); Allen's (coastal breeder)

Rare, casual, accidental: Broad-tailed, Broad-billed, Xantus'

Favored flowers: wild currant, bottlebrush, eucalyptus, foxglove,
crabapple

Arrival of migrants: January to February, Rufous and Allen's; March,
Black-chinned; March to May, Calliope

Departure of migrants: staggered by species September to October

Southern California (including Santa Catalina Island)
Number of species reported: 12

Most common: Anna's (resident); Black-chinned (resident breeder);
Costa's (spring and summer); Rufous; Calliope; Allen's
(coastal and Channel Islands breeder); Broad-tailed (desert
mountains summer)

Rare, casual, accidental: Broad-billed, Blue-throated, Violet-
crowned, Ruby-throated, Xantus'

Favored flowers: wild currant, penstemons, phlox, chuparosa, coral
bells, fireweed, paintbrush, bottlebrush, eucalyptus, foxglove, crabapple, California fuchsia, century plant, twinberry (coastal), catchfly; in the mountains: columbine,
manzanitas, mountain pennyroyal, bush monkey flower,
pitcher sage

Arrival of migrants: January to February, Rufous, Allen's; mid to
late March, others

Departure of migrants: May for Calliope; other species staggered
through late October

Colorado
Number of species reported: 7

Most common: Broad-tailed (nests, mostly in mountains); Rufous,
Black-chinned (nests, mostly south and west in foothills
and canyons)

Rare, casual, accidental: Calliope, Blue-throated, Magnificent, Anna's

Favored flowers: Nelson's larkspur, pussywillow, penstemon (beard-tongue), columbine, paintbrush, scarlet gilia, thistle, clover

Arrival of migrants: late April, Broad-tailed and Black-chinned; mid-July, Rufous and Calliope

Departure of migrants: early September for all species

Connecticut

Number of species reported: 2

Most common: Ruby-throated

Rare, casual, accidental: Rufous

Favored flowers: jewelweed, cardinal flower, day lily, petunia, violet, columbine, honeysuckle, penstemon

Arrival of migrants: April (earliest), first week May average

Departure of migrants: mid-September average

Delaware

Number of species reported: 2

Most common: Ruby-throated

Rare, casual, accidental: Rufous

Favored flowers: trumpet vine, rose of sharon, jewelweed, field thistle

Arrival of migrants: May 1

Departure of migrants: September 11

District of Columbia

Number of species reported: 2

Most common: Ruby-throated

Rare, casual, accidental: Rufous (migrant)

Favored flowers: trumpet vine, Oswego tea, spotted jewelweed, cardinal flower, eastern red columbine, coral honeysuckle, bee balm, red salvia, scarlet sage, coral bells, impatiens

Arrival of migrants: earliest April 2; average April 29

Departure of migrants: latest October 28; average September 26

Florida

Number of species reported: 9

Most common: Ruby-throated (breeds)

Rare, casual, accidental: Rufous (known to winter); Black-chinned (known to winter); Calliope (known to winter); Cuban Emerald; Bahama Woodstar; Buff-bellied (known to winter); Broad-tailed; Allen's

Favored flowers: thistle, coral honeysuckle, cow-itch vine, cala-
mentha, honeysuckle, columbine, Japanese flowering
quince, scarlet sage, snapdragon, phlox, petunia, larkspur, lily, morning glory, nasturtium, azalea, cardinal
flower

Arrival of migrants: Ruby-throated, second week March

Departure of migrants: Ruby-throated, last week October

Georgia

Number of species reported: 6

Most common: Ruby-throated (nests)

Rare, casual, accidental: Rufous (known to winter); Black-chinned
(known to winter); Broad-tailed, Magnificent, Buff-
bellied

Favored flowers: honeysuckle, cardinal flower, salvia, trumpet
creeper, crossvine, nasturtium, columbine, mimosa, zinnia, buckeye, larkspur, hibiscus, mallow, shrimp plant

Arrival of migrants: March 30 (Atlanta earliest); south, March 5
earliest ever in 1945

Departure of migrants: October 15 (Atlanta latest); south Nov. 25
(1958); December 7, 1990, fat migrant Ruby-throated,
Atlanta area

Hawaii

No hummingbirds reported.

Idaho

Number of species reported: 5

Most common: Black-chinned, Rufous, Calliope, Broad-tailed

Rare, casual, accidental: Anna's

Favored flowers: wild hawthorne, brodeia, delphinium, camas,
lupine, chokecherry

Arrival of migrants: mid-May earliest

Departure of migrants: September 10 latest

Illinois

Number of species reported: 2

Most common: Ruby-throated

Rare, casual, accidental: Rufous

Favored flowers: honeysuckle, trumpet creeper, morning glory, bee
balm, phlox, petunia, geranium

Arrival of migrants: (Chicago area) April 1–17

Departure of migrants: (Chicago area) mid September to early
October

Indiana

Number of species reported: 2

Most common: Ruby-throated

Rare, casual, accidental: Rufous

Favored flowers: jewelweed, trumpet creeper, canna, honeysuckle, columbine

Arrival of migrants: (Bloomington area) May 2–10; earliest April 8

Departure of migrants: (Bloomington area) June 4 to October 6; latest, on a Christmas bird count.

Iowa

Number of species reported: 2

Most common: Ruby-throated

Rare, casual, accidental: Rufous

Favored flowers: columbine, jewelweed, trumpet vine, petunia, lily, gladiola

Arrival of migrants: April 25 (Webster City earliest); April 26 (Sioux City earliest); April 27 (Davenport earliest)

Departure of migrants: November 27 (Waterloo); November 20 (Ledges State Park); October 10 (Iowa City)

Kansas

Number of species reported: 6

Most common: Ruby-throated

Rare, casual, accidental: Rufous (rare); Broad-tailed (casual); Calliope, Black-chinned, and Magnificent (accidental)

Favored flowers: salvia, petunia, canna, lobelia, honeysuckle

Arrival of migrants: April 2, east; mid-July, west

Departure of migrants: October 24

Kentucky

Number of species reported: 2

Most common: Ruby-throated (breeds)

Rare, casual, accidental: Rufous (fall)

Favored flowers: trumpet vine, jewelweed, touch-me-not, morning glory

Arrival of migrants: March 29 earliest

Departure of migrants: November 18 latest

Louisiana

Number of species reported: 9

Most common: Ruby-throated (breeds; occasionally winters); Rufous (winters regularly); Black-chinned (winters); Buff-bellied (winters)

Rare, casual, accidental: Allen's, Broad-tailed, Anna's, Calliope, Broad-billed (Metairie November 1990)

Favored flowers: trumpet vine, Japanese honeysuckle, mimosa, coral honeysuckle, tropical sage, cardinal flower, red morning glory, shrimp plant, Mexican cigar, turk's cap, sultan's turban

Arrival of migrants: Ruby-throated earliest, February 26 (Metairie); Rufous, earliest June 26 (Baton Rouge); Black-Chinned earliest September 3 (Metairie); Buff-bellied October 12 earliest (Metairie)

Departure of migrants: Buff-bellied as late as May; Ruby-throated as late as mid-April; Black-chinned, as late as mid-April

Maine

Number of species reported: 2

Most common: Ruby-throated

Rare, casual, accidental: hypothetical Rufous (Orono 1957)

Favored flowers: honeysuckle, columbine, trumpet vine, apple, jewelweed; also tree sap

Arrival of migrants: April 29 earliest (Cousins Island)

Departure of migrants: early October latest (Blue Hill)

Maryland

Number of species reported: 2

Most common: Ruby-throated

Rare, casual, accidental: Rufous

Favored flowers: trumpet vine, Oswego tea, spotted jewelweed, cardinal flower, eastern red columbine, coral honeysuckle, bee balm, red salvia, scarlet sage, coral bells, impatiens

Arrival of migrants: earliest April 2; average April 29

Departure of migrants: latest October 28; average September 26

Massachusetts

Number of species reported: 3

Most common: Ruby-throated

Rare, casual, accidental: Allen's (Nantucket Island), Rufous

Favored flowers: trumpet vine, bee balm, fuchsia, jewelweed, Oswego tea, cardinal flower

Arrival of migrants: April 27 (Boston area)

Departure of migrants: September 17 (Boston area)

Michigan

Number of species reported: 2

Most common: Ruby-throated

Rare, casual, accidental: Rufous (hypothetical)

Favored flowers: columbine; apple, pear, and cherry blossoms; trumpet creeper

Arrival of migrants: Ruby-throated, April 19 Kalamazoo area (earliest)

Departure of migrants: Ruby-throated, October 11

Minnesota

Number of species reported: 2

Most common: Ruby-throated

Rare, casual, accidental: Rufous (migrant)

Favored flowers: fireweed, trumpet vine, jewelweed

Arrival of migrants: earliest north, April 30; south, April 12

Departure of migrants: latest north, October 9; south, October 28

Mississippi

Number of species reported: 6

Most common: Ruby-throated

Rare, casual, accidental: Rufous, Buff-bellied, Black-chinned, Allen's, Calliope

Favored flowers: salvia, coral honeysuckle, red honeysuckle, impatiens, nasturtium, lily, geranium

Arrival of migrants: Ruby-throated, second week in March

Departure of migrants: Ruby-throated, October; other species, September through February

Missouri

Number of species reported: 3

Most common: Ruby-throated

Rare, casual, accidental: Rufous, Allen's

Favored flowers: trumpet vine, salvia, phlox, petunia, bee balm, columbine, shrimp plant, impatiens

Arrival of migrants: March 23 (Hollister)

Departure of migrants: November 2–3 (Springfield)

Montana

Number of species reported: 5

Most common: Calliope (nests conifer forest edge and streamside vegetation); Rufous (common in early post-fire habitat); Black-chinned (riparian habitat)

Rare, casual, accidental: Anna's, Broad-tailed

Favored flowers: honeysuckle, Indian paintbrush, rose, dogwood, hawthorne, serviceberry, penstemon

Arrival of migrants: Calliope and Rufous, May 16; Black-chinned, May 25

Departure of migrants: generally leave first week September

Nebraska

Number of species reported: 4

Most common: Ruby-throated (breeds in eastern part of state)

Rare, casual, accidental: Rufous, Broad-tailed, Calliope

Favored flowers: columbine, jewelweed

Arrival of migrants: April 7 earliest

Departure of migrants: October 8 latest

Nevada

Number of species reported: 9

Most common: Black-chinned; Anna's (year-round south); Broad-tailed (mountains); Rufous; Calliope; Costa's

Rare, casual, accidental: Allen's, Magnificent, Broad-billed

Favored flowers: manzanita, thistle, penstemon, redbud, locust, cactus blooms, various garden flowers

Arrival of migrants: mid-March for the Broad-tailed; other species follow

Departure of migrants: mid-August for Black-chinned and Costa's, with others leaving through mid-September

New Hampshire

Number of species reported: 2

Most common: Ruby-throated

Rare, casual, accidental: Rufous

Favored flowers: honeysuckle, cardinal flower, morning glory, lily, trumpet creeper, bee balm, impatiens, petunia, columbine, jewelweed, phlox, azalea, flowering quince

Arrival of migrants: April 22 (earliest)

Fall departure of migrants: most are gone by third week in September; latest is early October

New Jersey

Number of species reported: 3

Most common: Ruby-throated

Rare, casual, accidental: Rufous; Allen's

Favored flowers: bee balm, Oswego tea, trumpet creeper, honeysuckle, mimosa, cardinal flower, coral bells, jewelweed, day lily, turk's cap lily, lobelia, four-o-clock, delphinium, impatiens, geranium, Mexican sunflower, nasturtium, obedient plant, petunia, phlox, scarlet sage, flowering nicotiana, wild bergamot, zinnia, clematis, Japanese honeysuckle, morning glory, scarlet runner bean; many shrubs

Arrival of migrants: April 31, earliest; May 3–10 normal

Departure of migrants: October 15 latest; September 24–30 normal

New Mexico

Number of species reported: 13

Most common: Black-chinned, Broad-tailed, Rufous, Calliope

Rare, casual, accidental: Broad-billed, Violet-crowned, Costa's, Anna's, Magnificent, Ruby-throated, Blue-throated, White-eared, Lucifer

Favored flowers: trumpet vine, honeysuckle, cactus blooms, apple, coral bells, thistle, penstemon, columbine, Mexican campion, Century plant, Indian paintbrush

Arrival of migrants: Sapillo Valley (30 miles North of Silver City): earliest, March 22, Broad-tailed; April 1, Magnificent and Black-chinned; April 5, Blue-throated; June 26, Rufous; July 28, Calliope

Albuquerque (Rio Grande Valley): earliest, April 2, Black-chinned; April 8, Broad-tailed; July 14, Rufous; July 13, Calliope

Chama-Brazos-Los Ojos: earliest, April 15, Broad-tailed; May 1, Black-chinned; May 14, Blue-throated; June 22, Rufous; mid-June, Calliope

Departure of migrants: Chama-Brazos-Los Ojos: latest, Black-chinned October 4; Broad-tailed, September 20; Rufous, September 15; Calliope, September 15

Albuquerque (Rio Grande Valley): latest, September 18, Calliope; September 30, Rufous; October 3, Broad-tailed; October 5, Black-chinned.

Sapillo Valley (30 miles north of Silver City): August 17, Magnificent; September 15, Calliope; October 1, Rufous; October 4, Broad-tailed; mid-October, Black-chinned

Note: Anna's overwintered Las Cruces 5 successive years, including 1990.

New York

Number of species reported: 2

Most common: Ruby-throated

Rare, casual, accidental: Rufous

Favored flowers: tropical salvia, red bee balm, cardinal flower, fuchsia, jewelweed, trumpet vine, bromeliads, petunia, hibiscus; sapsucker holes

Arrival of migrants: Ruby-throated, mid to late April

Departure of migrants: early November

North Carolina
Number of species reported: 4

Most common: Ruby-throated

Rare, casual, accidental: Rufous; Green Violet-eared (one record); Black-chinned suspected but not confirmed

Favored flowers: trumpet creeper, cardinal flower, coral honeysuckle, Japanese honeysuckle, jewelweed

Arrival of migrants: early April; a few Ruby-throats overwinter; a few Black-chinned may overwinter, but are not confirmed.

Departure of migrants: late September into late October

North Dakota
Number of species reported: 1

Most common: Ruby-throated (nests, mostly along rivers NE)

Rare, casual, accidental: none reported

Favored flowers: spotted touch-me-not, columbine, gooseberry, raspberry

Arrival of migrants: early June

Departure of migrants: mid to late August

Ohio
Number of species reported: 2

Most common: Ruby-throated

Rare, casual, accidental: Rufous

Favored flowers: scarlet bergamot, red azalea, columbine, trumpet creeper, gladiola, dahlia, coral bells, clematis, cardinal flower (A packet of Hummingbird Garden Seeds is available from Ohio Dept. of Natural Resources.)

Arrival of migrants: April 16 earliest to May 7 (Cleveland area)

Departure of migrants: October 27 latest (Cleveland area)

Oklahoma
Number of species reported: 4

Most common: Ruby-throated (breeds in all but panhandle); Black-chinned (breeds in panhandle and far western counties).

Rare, casual, accidental: Rufous and Calliope, both late summer to early fall migrants

Favored flowers: impatiens, honeysuckle, salvia, coral bells, columbine, hibiscus, red bee balm, petunia, trumpet vine,
mimosa

Arrival of migrants: Claremore area, April 16 (earliest)

Departure of migrants: Grove area, October 5 (latest)

Oregon (West)

Number of species reported: 6

Most common: Rufous (summer); Anna's (summer and winter);
Calliope (summer)

Rare, casual, accidental: Black-chinned; Costa's (Portland); Allen's

Favored flowers: foxglove, gilia, red flowering currant, orange
honeysuckle, twinberry, Indian pink, hedge nettle, California fuchsia, columbine, larkspur, paintbrush, early
paintbrush

Arrival of migrants: Rufous, average March 4, earliest February 19

Departure of migrants: Rufous, early September (September 9 at
Corvallis)

Oregon (East)

Number of species reported: 5

Most common: Rufous, Calliope, Black-chinned

Rare, casual, or accidental: Anna's, Broad-tailed

Favored flowers: golden currant, serviceberry, river hawthorne,
syringa, lupine, Indian paintbrush, penstemons, chokecherry, wild currant, gooseberry

Arrival of migrants: February 14

Departure of migrants: December 29 (data: Merlin Eltzroth)

Pennsylvania

Number of species reported: 2

Most common: Ruby-throated (breeds)

Rare, casual, or accidental: Rufous (fewer than five recordings)

Favored flowers: scarlet quince, jewelweed, honeysuckle, trumpet
vine, salvia, monarda, petunia, impatiens

Arrival of migrants: April 10 (earliest)

Departure of migrants: September 20 through late October

Rhode Island

Number of species reported: 1

Most common: Ruby-throated

Rare, casual, accidental: none reported

Favored flowers: flowering quince (exotic), cardinal flower, jewelweed, monarda (exotic), trumpet creeper

Arrival of migrants: rarely before May 1
Departure of migrants: rarely after September 30

South Carolina
Number of species reported: 2

Most common: Ruby-throated

Rare, casual, or accidental: Rufous

Favored flowers: jewelweed, bee balm, red buckeye

Arrival of migrants: late March (males) to mid–April (females)

Departure of migrants: mid-September (males) to mid-October (females and immatures)

South Dakota
Number of species reported: 4

Most common: Ruby-throated east of Missouri River; Rufous west of the Missouri River

Rare, casual, or accidental: Broad-tailed, Calliope

Favored flowers: gilia, snapdragon, lemon mint, Canada thistle, coral bells, trumpet vine, zinnia, petunia

Arrival of migrants: May 17

Departure of migrants: latest west of the Missouri River, October 29; average August 1–21

Tennessee
Number of species reported: 2

Most common: Ruby-throated (breeds)

Rare, casual, or accidental: Rufous

Favored flowers: honeysuckle, trumpet vine, red buckeye, columbine

Arrival of migrants: Memphis, March 25 earliest, April 1 average; Nashville, March 24 earliest, April 15 average

Departure of migrants: Memphis, November 27 latest; November 1 average; Nashville, December 3 latest; October 10 average

Texas
Number of species reported: 19

Most common: Ruby-throated, Black-chinned, Broad-tailed, Anna's, Rufous, Magnificent, Lucifer, Buff-bellied, Blue-throated

Rare, casual, or accidental: Costa's, Green Violet-eared, Allen's, Calliope, Broad-billed, Violet-crowned, White-eared, Green-breasted Mango, Antillean Crested, Rufous-tailed

East Texas (Nacogdoches)

Number of species reported: 4

> *Most common:* Ruby-throated (common breeder)
>
> *Rare, casual, or accidental:* Rufous (rare migrant); Black-chinned; Anna's (1 recorded)
>
> *Favored flowers:* shrimp plant, live oaks, trumpet vine, honeysuckle, turk's cap
>
> *Arrival of migrants:* males March 15; females April
>
> *Departure of migrants:* October 20 latest

West Texas (El Paso)

Number of species reported: 14

> *Most common:* Black-chinned (breeds summer); Rufous (late summer, fall migrant); Broad-tailed (fall migrant); Calliope (late summer migrant); Anna's (winter resident); Lucifer (breeds Big Bend area); White-eared; Allen's
>
> *Rare, casual, or accidental:* Broad-billed, Blue-throated, Magnificent, Ruby-throated, Costa's, Violet-crowned
>
> *Favored flowers:* trumpet vine, penstemon, century plant, desert willow, Rocky Mountain beeplant, yucca
>
> *Arrival of migrants:* March 10
>
> *Departure of migrants:* mid-September

Central Texas (Austin)

Number of species reported: 9

> *Most common:* Ruby-throated, Austin area and east; Black-chinned, Austin area and west
>
> *Rare, casual, or accidental:* Rufous (fall migrant), Anna's, Broad-tailed, Costa's, Calliope, Allen's, Green Violet-eared
>
> *Favored flowers:* honeysuckle, turk's cap
>
> *Arrival of migrants:* April 5 (earliest)
>
> *Departure of migrants:* October 25 (average)

North Texas (Dallas/Fort Worth)

Number of species reported: 3

> *Most common:* Ruby-throated, Black-chinned
>
> *Rare, casual, or accidental:* Broad-tailed (fall migrant)
>
> *Favored flowers:* trumpet vine, cardinal flower
>
> *Arrival of migrants:* April 15
>
> *Departure of migrants:* September 20

South Texas (Coastal bend.)

Number of species reported: 13

> *Most common:* Ruby-throated (rare breeder, with an occasional

overwintering); Black-chinned (breeds, with a few overwintering); Rufous (a few overwintering)

Rare, casual, or accidental: Buff-bellied (breeds and winters in
Nuecus); Anna's; Calliope; Costa's; Green Violet-ear
(seen in Sinton in 1989); Lucifer; Broad-tailed; Blue-
throated; Broad-billed (recorded only once); Allen's

Favored flowers: turk's cap, trumpet vine, shrimp plant, firecracker
bush, coral honeysuckle, Mexican butterfly weed, Mexican honeysuckle, Mexican bush sage, Mexican cigar plant,
Hall's honeysuckle, salvia, scarlet sage, autumn sage, fire-
bush (Texas scarlet bush), desert willow, jacobinias, cape
honeysuckle, Lantana varieties

Arrival of migrants: Ruby-throated, March 8 earliest (Nueces);
Black-chinned, March 14 earliest (Nucces); Rufous, Au-
gust 22 earliest (Nueces); Anna's, December 26 earliest
(Nueces)

Departure of migrants: Ruby-throated, latest November 30 (Nueces);
Black-chinned, latest August 1 (Nueces); Anna's, latest
March 2 (Nueces); Rufous, latest March 24 (Nueces)

Texas Panhandle
Number of species reported: 6

Most common: Black-chinned (breeds); Ruby-throated (breeds eastern counties); Rufous (late summer migrant); Broad-tailed
(spring/fall migrant)

Rare, casual, or accidental: Calliope (late summer migrant); Anna's

Favored flowers: trumpet creeper, trumpet honeysuckle, clematis, mimosa, red yucca, bee balm, wild petunia, phlox,
parwinkle, columbine

Arrival of migrants: Amarillo, first week April, Black-chinned; late
May, Broad-tailed (passing through); July 16 (earliest)
Rufous; July 8 (earliest), Calliope

Departure of migrants: Amarillo, October 5, latest (Black-chinned)

Utah
Number of species reported: 9

Most common: Black-chinned, Broad-tailed, Calliope, Rufous,
Costa's (SW)

Rare, casual, or accidental: Anna's, Broad-billed, Magnificent, Blue-
throated

Favored flowers: honeysuckle, Eaton beard tongue, scarlet gilia,
Indian paintbrush, small and bearded beard tongue, tiger
lily, twinberry

Arrival of migrants: mid–April, northern Utah

Departure of migrants: mid to late September, northern Utah

Vermont

Number of species reported: 2

Most common: Ruby-throated

Rare, casual, or accidental: Rufous

Favored flowers: foxglove, lilac, dogwoods, bee balm, clematis, honeysuckle, impatiens, jewelweed, columbine, cardinal flower; also sapsucker holes

Arrival of migrants: April 24, earliest

Departure of migrants: October 26, latest

Virginia

Number of species reported: 2

Most common: Ruby-throated

Rare, casual, or accidental: Rufous

Favored flowers: trumpet creeper, trumpet honeysuckle, mimosa, jewelweed, four-o-clock

Arrival of migrants: April 20, Piedmont and coastal plain; April 25, ridge and valley

Departure of migrants: September 5, Piedmont; September 25, coastal plain; September 30, ridge and valley

Washington (West)

Number of species reported: 4

Most common: Rufous (breeds spring-summer); Anna's (breeds Seattle area early spring; winters rarely)

Rare, casual, or accidental: Black-chinned (south central); Calliope (suspected)

Favored flowers: salmonberry, columbine, penstemon, red currant, honeysuckle

Arrival of migrants: Rufous, last week February; Anna's, resident

Departure of migrants: Rufous, as late as mid-August

Washington (East)

Number of species reported: 3

Most common: Calliope (breeds); Black-chinned (breeds); Rufous (migrant)

Rare, casual, or accidental: none reported

Favored flowers: currants, Indian paintbrush, delphinium, Maltese cross, sage; tree sap of serviceberry

Arrival of migrants: April 11 (earliest)

Departure of migrants: late August

West Virginia

Number of species reported: ?

Most common: Ruby-throated

Rare, casual, or accidental: Rufous

Favored flowers: honeysuckle, begonia

Arrival of migrants: Huntington, April 19

Departure of migrants: Huntington, mid-September to late October

Wisconsin

Number of species reported: 3

Most common: Ruby-throated

Rare, casual, or accidental: Rufous, Anna's

Favored flowers: trumpet vine, jewelweed, fireweed, columbine, honeysuckle, petunia, lily

Arrival of migrants: early April, Ruby-throated, June-July, Rufous

Departure of migrants: mid-October

Wyoming

Number of species reported: 6

Most common: Broad-tailed (breeds); Calliope (breeds west)

Rare, casual, or accidental: Rufous (migrant); Black-chinned (migrant, mostly NW); Ruby-throated (migrant, mostly NE); Magnificent

Favored flowers: fireweed, Indian paintbrush, petunia, delphinium, columbine, gaillardias

Arrival of migrants: Broad-tailed, April 28; Calliope, May 13; Ruby-throated, May 14; Black-chinned, May 15; Rufous, June 14

Departure of migrants: Black-chinned, August 14; Ruby-throated, September 9; Calliope, September 12; Rufous, September 14; Broad-tailed, September 16

Canada

Alberta

Number of species reported: 3

Most common: Ruby-throated (breeds SE, central, and Peace River district); Rufous (migrant spring and summer)

Rare, casual, or accidental: Calliope (rare breeder in mountains from Waterton Lakes to Jasper)

Favored flowers: salmonberry, phlox, red flowering currant, squaw currant, petunia, Indian paintbrush, fireweed, honeysuckle

Arrival of migrants: earliest May 20

Departure of migrants: August

British Columbia

Number of species reported: 6

Most common: Rufous, Calliope, Black-chinned, Anna's (Victoria resident)

Rare, casual, or accidental: Costa's, Ruby-throated

Favored flowers: salmonberry, red-flowering currant, squaw currant, Indian paintbrush; all species feed extensively at sapsucker wells.

Arrival of migrants: coastal area: Rufous, earliest March 10, latest April 6. Interior: Rufous, earliest April 15, latest May 7; Calliope, April 7 to May 4; Black-chinned, earliest May 2

Departure of migrants: coastal area: Rufous, latest October 10. Interior: Rufous, latest October 31; Calliope, latest October 22; Black-chinned, September 4

Vancouver Island, BC

Number of species reported: 6

Most common: Rufous (widely distributed); Anna's (Victoria resident, otherwise east coast from Victoria to Campbell River); Costa's (Victoria to Nanaimo); Ruby-throated (Campbell River)

Rare, casual, or accidental: Calliope; Allen's (Victoria accidental)

Favored flowers: salmonberry, columbine, red-flowering currant, arbutus tree, big-leaf maple, honeysuckle, blueberry, huckleberry, thimbleberry

Arrival of migrants: earliest March 4, with peak from late March to early April

Departure of migrants: latest October 17, with peak from late August through early September

Manitoba

Number of species reported: 2

Most common: Ruby-throated

Rare, casual, or accidental: Rufous

Favored flowers: climbing honeysuckle, fireweed, delphinium, caragana, honeysuckle

Arrival of migrants: May 15

Departure of migrants: last week September

State and Province Species List

New Brunswick
Number of species reported: 1
Most common: Ruby-throated

Rare, casual, or accidental: none reported

Favored flowers: jewelweed, blackberry, apple, rhododendron, fuchsia, red monarda, Maltese cross

Arrival of migrants: April 17–19, earliest

Departure of migrants: November 6, latest

Newfoundland
Number of species reported: 2
Most common: Ruby-throated

Rare, casual, or accidental: Rufous (two summer records)

Favored flowers: bee balm, honeysuckle

Arrival of migrants: May 16, earliest

Departure of migrants: October 28, latest

Northwest Territories
Number of species reported: 1
Most common: Ruby-throated

Rare, casual, or accidental: none reported

No report of favored flowers or arrival or departure of migrants.

Nova Scotia
Number of species reported: 3
Most common: Ruby-throated

Rare, casual, or accidental: Rufous (three sightings); Black-chinned

Favored flowers: jewelweed, apple, rhododendron, maple, impatiens, columbine, fuchsia, red monarda

Arrival of migrants: April 19, earliest

Departure of migrants: October 23, latest

Ontario
Number of species reported: 5
Most common: Ruby-throated (breeds)

Rare, casual, or accidental: Rufous, Broad-billed (1989), Black-chinned (1990), Green Violet-eared (1991)

Favored flowers: delphinium, jewelweed, phlox, petunia, fireweed, geranium, honeysuckle, begonia, evening primrose

Arrival of migrants: Ontario, (earliest) early April; North Bay, May 1

Departure of migrants: Ontario, (latest) mid-November; North Bay, September 22

Prince Edward Island

Number of species reported: 1

Most common: Ruby-throated (breeds)

Rare, casual, or accidental: none reported

Favored flowers: impatiens, horse chestnut, lilac; sapsucker drillings
in maples

Arrival of migrants: May 20, average

Departure of migrants: October 1, latest

Quebec

Number of species reported: 1

Most common: Ruby-throated (breeds)

Rare, casual, or accidental: none reported

Favored flowers: clover, touch-me-not

Arrival of migrants: May 9–14

Departure of migrants: most gone by September 25, October 14
latest

Saskatchewan

Number of species reported: 4

Most common: Ruby-throated (breeds)

Rare, casual, or accidental: Calliope, Rufous (both stragglers); Black-
chinned (hypothetical)

Favored flowers: impatiens, geranium, petunia, lily, bee balm,
phlox, penstemons, lilac, honeysuckle, columbine, nasturtium, zinnia

Arrival of migrants: May 16–23

Departure of migrants: September 12–18

Yukon

Number of species reported: 1

Most common: Rufous (extreme southwest)

Rare, casual, or accidental: none reported

Favored flowers: no report

Arrival of migrants: late April to early May

Departure of migrants: early October

Bibliography

Albuquerque Tribune. 1992. May 16, A2.

American Scientist. 1990. July–August.

Andrews, D.F., and W.H. Baltosser. 1989. First record of Allen's hummingbird east of Louisiana. *Am. Birds* 43:429–30.

Arnold, L.W. 1930. Anna's hummingbird. *Bulletin 176, United States National Museum* 372.

Ashman, P. 1977. Northern (Bullock's) oriole eats hummingbird. *Western Birds* 8:105.

Atlanta Journal and Constitution. 1990. Atlanta still hot as hummer haven. Dec. 16 R1.

Austin, O.L., Jr. 1928. Migration—routes of the Arctic Tern (*Sterna paradisaea*).

Bakus, G.J. 1962. Early nesting of the Costa hummingbird in southern California. *Condor* 64:438.

Baltosser, W.H. 1986. Nesting success and productivity of hummingbirds in southwestern New Mexico and southwestern Arizona. *Wilson Bull.* 98(3):353–67.

———1987. Age, species, and sex determination of four North American Hummingbirds. *North American Bird Bander*, 12 (4): 151–66.

———1989. Costa's hummingbird: Its distribution and status. *Western Birds* 20(2):41–62.

———1989. Nectar availability and habitat selection by hummingbirds in Guadalupe Canyon. *Wilson Bull.* 101(4):559–78.

Bellrose, F.C., and R.R. Graber. 1963. A radar study of the flight directions of nocturnal migrants. In *Proc XIII, Int. Ornithol. Congr.* 362–89.

Bené, F. 1942. The feeding and related behavior of hummingbirds. Vol. 9, No. 3, *Memoirs of the Boston society of natural history*. Boston: Charles T. Branford Co.

Bodine, M.L. 1928. *National Geographic*, June, 731–42.

Bowles, J.H. 1910. The Anna hummingbird. *Condor* 12:125–27.

Bull. of Oklahoma Ornithological Society 2:14–15.

Butler, C. 1949. Hummingbird killed by praying mantis. *Auk* 66:286.

Calder, W.A., III. 1987. Southbound through Colorado; Migration of Rufous hummingbird. *National Geographic Research and Explorer* 31:40–51.

———1989. Implications of recapture data for migration of the Rufous hummingbird in the Rocky Mountains. *Auk* 106:488–89.

———1991. Territorial hummingbirds. *Natl. Geogr. Res. and Expl.* 7(1):56–69.

Carpenter, F.L., D.C. Patton, and A.M. Hixon. 1983. Weight gain and adjustment of feeding territory size in migrant hummingbirds. *Proc. Natl. Acad. Sci.* 80:7259–63.

Colwell, R.K., and S. Naeem. 1979. The first known species of hummingbird flower mite north of Mexico. *Rhinoseius epoecus*, n.sp. *Entom. Soc. of Amer.* 72(4):485–91.

Conway, A.E., and S.R. Drennan. 1979. Rufous hummingbirds in eastern North America. *Am. Birds* 33:130–32.

Des Grange, J.L. 1979. Organization of a tropical nectar feeding bird guild in a variable environment. *Living Bird* 17:199–236.

Demaree, S.R. 1970. Nest-building, incubation period, and fledgling in the Black-chinned hummingbird. *Wilson Bull.* 82:225.

DuBois, A.D. 1939. Observations at a Rufous hummingbird's nest. *Auk* 55: 629–41.

Edgerton, H.E. 1947. Hummingbirds in action. *National Geographic*, Aug., 220–32.

———1987. *Electronic flash, strobe*. McGraw-Hill.

Bibliography

Feinsinger, P. 1988. Mixed support for spatial heterogeneity in species interactions: hummingbirds in a tropical disturbance mosaic. *Amer. Nat.* 131(1)33–57.

Feinsinger, P., and S.B. Chaplin. 1975. Wing disc loading and foraging in hummingbirds. *Amer. Nat.* 109:217–24.

Fox, R.P. 1954. Plumages and Territorial behavior of the Lucifer hummingbird in the Chisos mountains, Texas. *Auk* 71:465–66.

Gamboa, G.J. 1977. Predation of Rufous hummingbird by Wied's flycatcher. *Auk* 94:157–58.

Gass, C.L. 1979. Territory regulation, tenure, and migrating in rufous hummingbirds. *Canadian Journal of Zoology* 57:914–23.

Gessell, J.P. 1934. Ruby-throated hummingbird. *Bird-Lore* 36:291–93.

Grant, J. 1955. Hummingbirds attacked by wasps. *Canadian Field-Naturalist* 73:174.

Greenewalt, C.H. 1960a. The hummingbird. *National Geographic*, Nov., 658–79.

————1960b. *Hummingbirds*. Garden City, N.Y.: Doubleday & Co.

————1963. Photographing hummingbirds in Brazil. *National Geographic*, Jan.

Hainesworth, F. Reed, and Larry Wolf. 1972. Flight power and hummingbird size. *Amer. Nat.* 106:589–95.

Hassler, S.S., R.R. Graber, and F.C. Bellrose. 1963. Fall migration and weather; a radar study. *Wilson Bull.* 75:56–77.

Hering, L. 1946. Courtship and mating of broad-tailed hummingbirds in Colorado. *Condor* 49:126.

Hildebrand, E.M. 1949. Hummingbird captured by a praying mantis. *Auk* 66:286.

Hixon, M.A., and F.L. Carpenter. 1988. Distinguishing energy maximizers from time minimizers: A comparative study of two hummingbird species. *Amer. Zool.* 28:913–25.

Inouye, D.W., W.A. Calder, and N.M. Waser. 1991. The effect of floral abundance on feeder censuses of hummingbird populations. *Condor* 93:279–85.

Johnsgard, P.A. 1983. *The hummingbirds of North America*. Washington, D.C. Smithsonian Institution Press.

Kuban, J.F., and R.L. Neill, 1980. Feeding ecology of hummingbirds in the highlands of the Chisos Mountains, Texas. *Condor* 82:180–85.

Lasiewski, R.C. 1962. The energetics of migrating hummingbirds. *Condor* 64(4):324.

Lowery, G.H., Jr. 1938. Hummingbird in a pigeon hawk's stomach. *Auk* 55:280.

Lyon, D.L. 1976. A montane hummingbird territorial system in Oaxaca, Mexico. *Wilson Bull.* 88:280–99.

Mayr, E. 1966. Hummingbird caught by sparrow hawk. *Auk* 83:664.

Mayr E. and L.L. Short, Jr. 1970. Species taxa of North American birds: A contribution to comparative systematics. *Publ. Nuttall Orinthol. Club* 9:1–127.

Miller, A.H., and R.C. Stebbins. 1964. *The Lives of Desert Animals in Joshua Tree National Monument*. Berkeley: University of California Press.

Miller, S.J., and D.W. Inouye. 1983. Roles of the wing whistle in the territorial behavior of male broad-tailed hummingbirds. *American Behav.* 31:689–700.

Monroe, M. 1957. Hummingbird killed by a frog. *Condor* 59:69.

Moore, R.T. 1939a. Habits of white eared hummingbirds. *Auk* 56:442–46.

————1939b. The Arizona broad-billed hummingbird. *Auk* 56:313–19.

News, The. 1991a. Forests' fate hanging on ejido reform. December 11. Mexico City.

————1991b. Assembly unsure of position on campesino protest threat. December 18. Mexico City.

————1991c. Megaproject raises ecology fears. December 15. Mexico City.

Nickell, W.P. 1948. Alternate care of two nests by a Ruby-throated hummingbird. *Auk* 60:242–43.

Norris-Elye, L.S.T. 1944. Leopard frogs devouring small birds. *Auk* 61:643–44.

Bibliography

Orr, R.T. 1939. Observations on the nesting of the Allen hummingbird. *Condor* 41:17–24.

Pearson, O.P. 1960. *Speed of the Allen hummingbird while diving.* Museum of Vertebrate Zoology, Berkeley, California.

Peters, H.J. 1963. Two observations on avian predation. *Wilson Bull.* 75:274.

Peters, S.J. 1991. To catch a hummingbird. *Explorer*, Fall 1991. The Cleveland Museum of Natural History.

Phillips, A. R. 1965. Notas sistematicas sobre aves Mexicanas. *III Rev. Soc. Mex. Hist. Nat.*, 217–42.

————1975. The migrations of Allen's and other hummingbirds. *Condor* 77:196–205.

Prowse, E.L. 1934. Our hummingbirds. *Bird-Lore* 36:232–36.

Russell, S.M. and D.W. Lamm. 1978. Notes on the distribution of birds in Sonora, Mexico. *Wilson Bull* 90:123–30.

Skutch, A.E. 1973. *The Life of the Hummingbird.* Crown Publishing, Inc.

Spofford, S.H. 1976. Roadrunner catches hummingbird in flight. *Condor* 78:142.

Sprot, G.D. 1925–26. Rufous hummingbird. *Bulletin 176, United States National Museum* 398.

Stiles, F.G. 1978. Possible specialization for hummingbird hunting in the tiny hawk. *Auk* 95:550–53.

Stong, C.L. 1960. Does a hummingbird find its way to nectar through its sense of smell? *Scientific Amer.* 202(2):157–66.

Stott, K. 1951. An Anna hummingbird caught in a spider web. *Condor* 53:49.

Stromberg, M.R., and P.B. Johnson. 1990. Hummingbird sweetness preferences: Taste or viscosity? *Condor* 92:606–12.

Tamm, S. 1985. Breeding territory quality and agonistic behavior: effects of energy availability and intruder pressure in hummingbirds. *Behav. Ecol. Sociobiol.* 16: 203–7.

Thompson, A.L. 1960. Bird-migration terms. *Ibis* 102:140.

Trousdale, B. 1954. Copulation of Anna hummingbirds. *Condor* 56:110.

True, D. 1980. *A family of eagles.* Everest House.

————1984. *Flying Free.* Dodd, Mead and Co.

————1993. A history of hummingbird feeders. *Hummingbirds of North America: Attracting, Feeding, and Photographing.* Albuquerque: University of New Mexico Press.

Wagner, H.O. 1955. The molt of hummingbirds. *Auk* 72:286–91.

Waldvogel, J.A. 1990. The bird's eye view. *American Scientist* 78:342–53.

Weis-Fogh, T. 1972. Energetics of hovering flight in hummingbirds and in drosophilia. *Journal of Experimental Biology* 56:79–104.

Wells, S., R.A. Bradley, and L.F. Baptista. 1978. Hybridization in *Calypte* hummingbirds. *Auk* 95:537–49.

Weydemeyer, W. 1927. Notes on the location and construction of the nest of the calliope hummingbird. *Condor* 24:19–24.

Willimont, L.A., S.E. Senner, and Goodrich. 1988. Fall migration of Ruby throat hummingbirds in the northeastern United States. *Wilson Bull.* 100:482–88.

Woods, R.S. 1927. The hummingbirds of California. *Auk* 44:297–318.

————1931. Hummingbird boarders. *Condor* 33:181–87.

————1934. A hummingbird entangled in a spider web. *Condor* 36:242.

Wright, B.S. 1962. Baltimore oriole kills hummingbird. *Auk* 79:112.

Wyman, L.E. 1920. Calliope hummingbird. *Bulletin 176, United States National Museum* 422–23.

Index

Index

Index

Index

Index

Index